"THE FUNNIEST BOOK ABOUT WINE...EVER!"
Jerry Henry, *WWL Radio, New Orleans*

"In the wonderful, but complex world of wine, there is nobody like Jake Lorenzo. Nobody. He is our Henry Miller, our Paul Gauguin, our Robin Williams."
Bob Sessions, *Hanzell Vineyards*

"When your typical wine writer is worrying about which advertiser not to offend, Mr. Lorenzo is telling the truth. He is to writing what 'rap' is to Tin Pan Alley."
Palmer Smoux, *Borderline Magazine*

"If you want to laugh at the underbelly of politics, read Hunter S. Thompson. If you want to laugh at the underbelly of the wine business, read Jake Lorenzo."
Chuy Palacios, *The Burrito Palace*

"When entering Jake's world, be prepared to feel with your soul, and celebrate life without a safety net."
Momma Catherine, *Toonknocker Queen*

"Old Jake's conscience just keeps itching, and old Jake keeps on making a good show out of scratching it. Good, clear writing on some subjects that need to be talked about just like this."
Bob Thompson, *San Francisco Examiner*

"Nietzche borrowed Dionysus to symbolize genius, the force that encourages each one of us to respond to the world freely, in his or her own way. If he'd waited a while, he'd have had a better example: Jake Lorenzo."
Gerald Asher, *Gourmet Magazine*

"IF JAKE LORENZO DIDN'T EXIST, WE'D HAVE TO INVENT HIM."

Cyril Penn, *Wine Business Monthly*

"I always look forward to encounters with Jake Lorenzo. I never know what to expect, but that's part of the charm of knowing him. His down-to-earth style, his approach to life and his understanding of the intricacies of winemaking won me over."

Rusty Staub, *Baseball Legend*

"Each time I read a story by Jake Lorenzo, I feel as though he's grabbed me by the scruff of the neck and led me into a world of intrigue, cool cats, hip music, proverbs and, of course, wines galore."

Chris Sawyer, *WINE X Magazine*

"Forget the Wine Spectator, Wine Advocate or any traditional wine publication. Jake Lorenzo has created the book for people who are into wine and just enjoy a good read."

Ray Kaufman, *Laurel Glen Vineyards*

"Jake is a Renaissance man. I'd hate to have him as a client, because there is no telling what he might do, but *Further Surveillance* is a must read for anyone who wants to know about life in the wine business."

Michael Coats, *Coats Public Relations*

"One of the best books on the California wine business I've read."

Larry Walker, *Wine & Spirits Magazine*

"Discovering Jake Lorenzo is like inheriting a wine cellar where each and every bottle is perfectly aged. In fact, I find that Jake Lorenzo is even funnier and more perceptive if I'm drinking while reading."

Lance Cutler, *Relentless Vineyard*

FURTHER SURVEILLANCE

Underground Stories of the Wine Business

by
Jake Lorenzo

WINE PATROL PRESS FIRST EDITION, OCTOBER 2004

Library of Congress Catalogue Card Number: 200410638

Lorenzo, Jake. Further Surveillance: Underground Stories
of the Wine Business
by Jake Lorenzo.

—First Edition
p.cm

ISBN 0-9637438-6-4: $16.95 Softcover

Published by
Wine Patrol Press
P.O. Box 228
Vineburg, CA 95487 USA

Printed in the United States of America

*For Chloe and Cara, a bit of history
for the future generations*

ACKNOWLEDGEMENTS

Thanks to Bob Johnson who contributed the cover and a consistently twisted counsel that helped form this book.

Dave Ogaz sitting in his dark warren translated my work into good-looking print.

Paul Costigan, Debbie Bell and Lisa Weber for proof reading. Any mistakes are their fault.

Charles McCabe for the model and example of the true professional drinker.

Thanks to all the people who gave encouragement, advice, help and discounts in the editing, printing, and publishing of this book.

Thanks to all of the patrons whose generous pre-paid purchase of *Further Surveillance* raised the capital to proceed, and gave life to this book.

Finally, to Jakelyn and her Mom... Who knew?

CONTENTS

PART I: **MEET JAKE LORENZO**

Death Threats. 3

It's a Mystery 7

DJ Jake. 9

Humor. 13

Terror for the Taliban. 17

Moving On 19

Gimme a Jake. 23

PART II: **FAMILY, HOME AND HEARTH**

Weddings 29

Grandpa Jake 33

Environmental Factors. 37

More Than a Home. 41

Construction 45

Hard Times. 49

Hunting. 53

Labor Day 57

Grapevines and Grandbabies 61

Dad. 65

PART III: **ON THE ROAD**

Wine Tasting in Europe 71

Spanish Anniversary. 75

A Spanish Meal 79

In Hot Water 83

Oregon Vacation 87

Dreams and Consequences 91

The Tequila Life 95

The Stuff with the Worm 99

Minister of Culture 103

Garbage 107

Simple Pleasures 111

Jake Lorenzo's Guide to New Orleans 113

PART IV: MUSING WITH JAKE

Success Is Fleeting 121

The Court Case 125

A House Is Not Always a Home 129

Soothe the Savage Beast 133

Drunkenness 135

Dining Out 137

A Night in Baja Sonoma 141

The Best 145

Not for Sale 149

PART V: THE WINE INDUSTRY

Tribute 155

Bum's Rush 157

Greed and the American Way 161

The Cellar Rat Ball 165

Interrogation 169

Bigger Is Not Always Better 173

A Wild Hair Idea 177

PART I

MEET JAKE LORENZO

Death Threats

It's a Mystery

DJ Jake

Humor

Terror for the Taliban

Moving On

Gimme a Jake

DEATH THREATS

"Hello, is this Jake Lorenzo?"

I thought the voice sounded familiar. "Yeah, this is Jake Lorenzo. What can I do for you?"

"Mr. Lorenzo, this is Morley Safer. I think I have a little problem, and I'd like to hire you in your professional capacity to help solve it."

Safer was in San Francisco working on a *60 Minutes* story. He'd received a series of threatening notes. The notes had all been postmarked from Sonoma, California. When I asked where he'd heard of Jake Lorenzo, he replied, "Why, from *Cold Surveillance*, you sent me a copy after I did my first piece on the "French Paradox."

I got his address and headed for The City.

*   *   *

In person, Morley (as he likes to be called) has a huggable quality. All of those deep furrowed wrinkles you see on television take on a bloodhound quality, but his eyes twinkle with spirit and good humor. We had the notes spread on the table between us. There were three of them. Each consisted of words cut from magazines pasted onto plain, white paper.

The first note read, "Stop telling people wine is good for them, or you die."

The second admonished, "Cancel all future positive wine stories, or you'll be in permanent re-runs."

"It's that last note that caused me to call, Jake. It looks like blood down at the bottom."

The last note threatened, "Stop touting wine, or your 60 minutes are up, you slime sucking son of a bitch." There was a large, dried red spot at the bottom.

Morley was saying, "I'm a pretty visible person, Jake. I'd prefer this not go public. I've no desire to be the subject of so exploitative a story. That's why I've opted for your services instead of going to the police."

I studied the spot of blood.

"I suppose it could be someone from the religious right," continued Morley, "some sort of off-kilter teetoteler."

I sniffed at the blood spot.

"What do you want me to do, Jake?" asked Morley. "I can arrange for protection if you think it's necessary."

I tasted the spot of blood.

That stopped him. "Good God, man! What on earth are you doing?"

"Mr. Safer," I said, "you don't need to worry about this. Just go about your business. You won't be getting any more threats. I can guarantee it. You see, I know who sent these notes."

*   *   *

A contrite Chuy poured a fresh cup of coffee, added the requisite shot of Hornitos, and stared morosely at the three notes on the counter. "How did you know it was me, Jake?"

I tapped the blood spot on the third note. "I'd know red chili sauce from The Burrito Palace anywhere, carnal."

"Well, how am I supposed to know that a big shot TV star like Morley Safer is pals with Jake Lorenzo?" asked Chuy, with more than a touch of indignation.

"Maybe other people don't know that I actually do detective work, Chuy, but you've got no excuse. We've even worked on a few cases together. Why'd you do it Chuy? What the hell were you thinking?"

"Hell, Jake, you know me. I'm not serious about killing nobody, but somebody's got to do something. That Morley Safer and all his damn reports on how wine makes you healthy is screwing things up for us common men. He's got people sucking down vino like it was Ponce de Leon's fountain of youth.

"He's created *un gran tornado* that is sucking up every damn bottle of red wine in this country. The wineries keep raising their prices to slow the flow, but it don't work. There's no juice, people are standing in line for what's left, and the prices have gone through the roof.

"I'm a working man, Jake. You don't get rich selling rice and beans to gringos. Where am I supposed to get $20 to $30 for a bottle of red wine? Not only that, but the damn vino is being released too soon. It's full of new oak and young, green fruit. It's so soft and ready to drink, I get nervous that it will die before I empty my glass. I'm telling you, Jake, lots of people are going to be *mucho* disappointed in a few years when they taste some of this stuff they're piling into their cellars."

Chuy does have a point. I don't know that it's so directly linked to Morley Safer, but wine has become scarce, and prices have become ridiculous. I was up in Washington state last week. Washington wines have always amazed me. Except for a few of the larger wineries, you rarely see them in other parts of the United States. But in Washington, the wines are everywhere. Restaurants, wine shops, people's homes, Washington wines are the rage. Not just any Washington wine, but the "right ones". The wines nobody can find. The ones that cost a fortune.

Washingtonians are in a frenzy to buy these wines. One famous winery had just released its 1994 merlot. It was priced at more than $40 per bottle. Stores were limiting customers to one bottle each. Give me a break. I tasted that famous $40 dollar bottle of wine. There was one thing that was spectacular about it: how did they get *all that oak* into a 1994 merlot, and *still* have the wine in the store within seventeen months?

Jake Lorenzo is not picking on Washington. Across the country people are waiting in line to buy all kinds of high priced wines, especially if some magazine scores them at 90 or above. If it says "merlot" on the label, people will buy it, no matter what the cost or the taste. Wineries are out of stock. They're raising prices higher than the national debt. They're aging, bottling and shipping wines faster than Marvin Shanken can light a cigar. The French, Italians and Spanish are all raising prices to keep up. It makes a wine drinking detective wonder if the country has gone mad.

To Jake Lorenzo, this whole wine frenzy is like the Emperor's new clothes. You remember the story of an Emperor who hired a tailor. The tailor was to make a robe for the Emperor to wear at a big parade, only it was a scam. (Private eyes always recognize a scam.) There was no robe, but everyone was afraid to tell the Emperor. So the Emperor is riding in the parade, bare-ass naked, and people are all saying what a fine robe it is. They are all afraid to admit that they can't see the robe. Finally, some kid shouts out, "Hey, the Emperor's naked," and the spell was broken. People started laughing at the Emperor, and his highness was mightily embarrassed. (I doubt the tailor got much more work, but I hear he retired in Chile where wine is cheap.)

It's pretty much the same with this wine frenzy. All these kings are talking about these beautiful robes in the bottle. The people come to the parade and plunk down princely sums to buy these bottles. When they drink many of them, they find them lacking, naked of flavor and finesse. Afraid to admit they can't see the robe, they say, "This is fantastic. What wonderful wine. I'm so lucky to have it at any price."

Where's that little kid? Who's going to step up and say the bottle is empty? Don't make Jake do it. Not again.

Chuy's staring at the notes on the counter. He shakes his head. "It's dumb Jake, I can't believe I sent these."

"It's OK Chuy, at least when you called him a 'slime sucking son of a bitch' it had a beautiful alliterative quality," I said, trying to cheer him up.

"We've got to do something, Jake. If we don't slow down all this wine sales, we won't have no vino for ourselves."

"Don't worry, carnal, Jake is on the case." I reach into my pocket and pull out a press release. Chuy reads it, starts laughing, and brings me a beer. "Lunch is on me, Jake," he says and walks into the kitchen still chuckling.

I look down at the press release sitting on the counter next to Chuy's three notes.

WINE MAY DECREASE SEX DRIVE

Dr. Iggy Calamari, inventor of the wine-powered pacemaker, has just released a report to *The Journal of Medicine* describing a three-year study showing that regular consumption of wine may slow down the normal sex drive in both men and women. As little as one or two glasses of wine a day reduced sexual desire by more than 65%. "It seems to be a delayed reaction, and doesn't show up for the first six to eight months of regular wine consumption," said Dr. Calamari. "We must always remember that beneficial effects of certain agents can be offset by side effects."

IT'S A MYSTERY

Jake Lorenzo has been a private eye for more than 30 years, but there are still lots of unsolved mysteries. For example, where does my cat go when Jakelyn is visiting and brings her dog? She brings the damn dog into the house, and the cat disappears. Four, five, six days: the cat is nowhere. Jakelyn leaves with the dog, and within an hour the cat is on the porch meowing up a storm, complaining until she's fed.

And what is with these doctors changing priorities for liver transplants? I mean, Jake Lorenzo has spent a lifetime exercising my liver to the limits on a daily basis. I've been saving for that liver transplant operation for decades. I've picked out my own doctor and hospital in Chicago. I secured the deal by taking the whole transplant team to a Cub game where Rusty Staub had given me front row seats. I'm going to be incredibly pissed off if I go in for my transplant only to find my replacement liver has been shipped to some life-long abstainer who contracts a rare liver disease.

Do you ever wonder about gophers? Jake Lorenzo does. Those damn gophers will gobble down one tomato plant after another, but when I start to dig around looking for a main tunnel so I can poison the bastards, I never find the damn things. After a couple of hours, my garden looks like a war zone. Holes all over the place resembling craters from mortar shells, but I never find a main tunnel.

Because Jake Lorenzo is an officially recognized wine writer, I get lots of different wine publications sent to my house. This month alone, I've already received a *Wine Enthusiast* that lists and rates more than 400 cabernets. I also got the latest *Wine Advocate* from Robert Parker that rates hundreds of California's greatest wines. Most of these wines start at $20 and quickly go up to an average price of $35-$40, and then escalate to $70 and more. Who the hell is buying these wines?

I mean Jake Lorenzo is a very successful private eye, not to mention a world famous author, but I can't afford to spend $70-$80 a day for wine. (After all, two bottles a day is all we ask.) Not only that, but I'm getting older. Even with bifocals I have a hard time reading the fine print on a label. It drives me up a wall when I spend my money on a bottle of wine trying to support a local winery only to find that the wine has come in from Chile, Languedoc, or some fine vineyard in Tibet. Is there any California wine in any California wine bottles?

And how do wineries get their wine made so fast these days? I was in the local wine shop for Christmas and almost 20% of the wines were from the

1995 vintage. December of 1996, and 1995 red wines are on the market. Let's see, that means just 14 months ago those bottles were hanging on grapevines. What the hell are you doing, running the grapes through a microwave to speed up the aging? And where do you get the nerve to charge $30 for a baby rushed to market?

Why is everybody out of wine? Who the hell is buying the stuff, and is anybody drinking it? As a private eye, I am convinced that somewhere, perhaps buried in dilapidated missile silos left over from the cold war, millions and millions of cases of wine are sitting stored by wealthy collectors who have paid exorbitant prices for rare wines that no one ever actually gets to taste.

How come people don't go out for three hour lunches anymore? I think people in the wine business are obligated to go to restaurants and have large, multi-course lunches, where bottle after bottle of wine pile up on the table. Where conversation gets louder and louder, and laughter explodes throughout the room until any idea of returning to work becomes out of the question, and the only sensible idea is to find a cab to take you home.

Why is it that when you walk into a tasting room you can buy shirts, hats, books, videos, napkin rings, wine openers, calendars, condiments, and candy, but you're limited to a two bottle purchase if you want some wine?

Jake Lorenzo loves restaurants, but this wine pricing is getting out of hand. If you want to start your wine list at $30 per bottle and then escalate upwards like an Apollo mission, that's your business. Personally, the idea of having dinner with Jakelyn's mother where our bill for food comes to $35, but our tab for wine is $50, strikes me as ridiculous. Why can't you at least have a few great delicious wine bargains on every wine list for us working people who really love fine wine?

What ever happened to riesling? Back in the 1970's it was known as the king of white grapes. Only fine white burgundies could come close to the regal riesling. When was the last time you even saw one? If they are out there, I'll bet you can get them cheap.

How come every restaurant offers wine by the glass, but they so rarely have anything that I want and can afford to drink?

Why do we have a grape shortage, when grapes are being planted faster than nurseries can grow rootstocks?

How much does it cost to take an ad in a major wine publication these days, and why do people continue to do it?

Where are all the corkscrews lost by waiters?

Why do people insist on opening champagne with sabers?

Why do fools fall in love?

Jake Lorenzo doesn't have the answers. They remain unsolved mysteries, but I'll tell you one thing. Jake Lorenzo will never go drinking with Andy Rooney again.

DJ JAKE

Jake Lorenzo is a detective, a good one, so he knows how to sneak around. Good thing, because when Jakelyn's mother hears the reggae music pounding from the new speakers he's just installed on the porch, he'd better make himself scarce. The neighbor has already slammed her window shut, which Jake takes as a good sign. After all, she seems to slam that window shut two or three times a day. As far as Jake can tell, slamming the window shut is about the only exercise she gets. She sure ain't working out any muscles by smiling.

Jake Lorenzo loves music. In fact, music is an important tool for a detective. Too much of detective work is spent waiting for something to happen. Stakeouts are the worst. Talk about time dragging. Stakeouts are worse than an extra-inning one run baseball game in July. The only way to bear stakeouts is put your very fine car audio system to use.

Listening to music in your car, especially when you're not going anywhere allows for a wide range of musical genres. It all depends on Jake's mood. Any kind of jazz from Louis to Miles to Dizzy is just fine. Old R&B is fun and helps pass the time. Funky New Orleans beats will help keep you going into the wee hours. When you're actually moving in the car, especially on long road trips, that's the perfect time for those compilation tapes. Doesn't matter what the theme, the surprise of each succeeding tune accentuates the new territory flying by outside your window. Classic rock and roll is always good on the road. Nothing like power chords and meandering guitar solos to eat up the miles.

Certain jobs cry out for specific types of music. I don't think you can produce a decent pot of red beans, if you're not playing zydeco. I mean you can do it in Louisiana, but not out here on the left coast. Play corridos and mariachi music while you're making a fine Mexican dinner and the food will taste a lot better.

Rap music is perfect for working out and pounding the weights. The base thump acts like a metronome for your heart, and all that talk about booty reminds you why you're working up a sweat in the first place. I love linking rap music with exercise. Since Jake Lorenzo doesn't exercise, he doesn't listen to much rap music. It's a perfect world. The only rap music I listen to regularly is from the cars that park across the street while they run in to get whatever packages they require for their weekend entertainment. I try to lie flat on my worktable. That way the vibrating bass pounding from their giant speakers acts like a magic fingers on my back, which is as close as Jake

Lorenzo wants to get to exercise anyway.

Jake Lorenzo believes that you can't make wine without good music. During harvest time, it's all about the beat. Most of us are charged up enough with the thrill of crush, so something that has plenty of energy with an easy, repetitive groove is perfect. Jake Lorenzo especially likes African music during crush. Try playing some King Sunny Ade when you're setting up in the morning. It's like meditating. Later in the afternoon, brighten things up with Mahlathini and the Mahotella Queens. You'll be dancing while you run the crusher, and a cold beer will taste like honey. Clean up with some Johnny Clegg and the grapes will roll happily to the drains. On the other hand, you may not like African music. Maybe you were an elephant in an earlier life, and you never forgave a tribesman for taking your ivory tusks. So, to this very day, the heart-beating thump of a talking drum fills your soul with dread.

You see, that's the problem with music in the workplace. Music is not necessarily democratic. Someone has to be in charge. Someone has to make decisions and take responsibility for the results. Now that most wineries are owned by corporate giants of one kind or another, getting music into a winery is tough. There are all the forms to fill out, the committees to review the music choices, and the attorneys to make sure nothing is carried over the speakers that might upset the visitors. There's the expense of carpenters who have to build the sound room and electricians to wire the stereo components and mount the speakers. There are the special meetings to vote on the playlists, the purchase orders, the delivery receipts to sign, and the rubber gloves to buy when opening the CD packages so no one gets hurt.

Then there's the whole issue of volume. Jake Lorenzo says that louder is better, within reason. Jakelyn's mom says, "Whatever you've got that at, it's too loud."

In the new corporate winery situation, you've got to deal with the OSHA inspectors, the sound technicians, the county supervisors, and the new neighbors who seemingly moved to the wine country just to complain about the groan of tractors, the whine of pneumatic presses, and the clouds of sulfur dust. They sure as hell don't want to be listening to African music while they sip their gin and tonics pool side. I say give all of those neighbors a window they can slam shut, and be done with them.

It's all another reason to spend your hard-earned dollars on wine produced at small wineries. Those little three and four man operations never seem to have arguments about the music. CDs and tapes sit in messy piles, often splattered with lees, and whoever is closest changes the music when they sicken of the current selection. They're in tune with the work of making fine wine, and the wine is created in a musical environment that is simple, pleasant, and exhilarating, all at the same time.

Music is also important when you're drinking wine, and it makes a great gift. Think about it. You get invited to someone's house for dinner. Don't bring a bottle of wine; tell them you're bringing the music. After all, they're already in the wine business. They need another bottle of wine like Jess Jackson needs another winery. But music, now you're talking.

Sit down with your old stereo equipment and make a compilation tape. Or if you must, work at your computer and burn a compilation disc. Producing a compilation tape or CD is easy; it's choosing the actual music and the order of the songs that will kill you. But it only takes time, and it's time well spent. All of us are too busy nowadays. Force yourself to take a few hours and make a tape. Draw a really neat cover and color it brightly. Give it a great title like *Jake Lorenzo Divests* (African music), *Jake Lorenzo's a Rude Boy* (Dub based reggae), or *Jake's Got Nothing to Say* (instrumental).

When you arrive for dinner, hand your creation to the host and say. "I brought this for the evening. Hope you like it." Then don't say anything else about it. It's up to the host to play it or not, and the worst thing you can do is keep interrupting conversation or drinking to point out songs or musical trivia.

Right now it's hotter than hell, but Jake Lorenzo has just met deadline. I'm sending this off to my editor, and then I'm mixing a tall tequila and squirt, and I'm going to sit on my new porch, crank up some reggae, and see if I can get my neighbor to slam her window shut.

HUMOR

Jake Lorenzo is not a procrastinator. I am lazy. I often screw around the whole day, accomplishing very little, but I am not a procrastinator.

Jake Lorenzo has been writing articles for *Practical Winery and Vineyards* for more than 20 years. Occasionally, I'll be traveling or working a case and I'll miss my deadline, but that happens rarely.

About eight weeks ago, I wrote a column. An inspired column, it still makes me laugh. I sent it into the magazine, weeks ahead of deadline. (I told you Jake is not a procrastinator.) A few days later I received a notification from the editor. My column had been rejected. I was crushed. Well, not crushed exactly, I was exasperated. I mean after twenty years, you'd think they'd cut me a little slack. At least, they could have called and discussed it with me. But they opted to send a fax, sort of an electronic rejection letter like the ones I keep getting from publishers for all of my books.

Granted, in the past, *Practical Winery and Vineyards* has expressed some concern regarding my eclectic topics. They pretty much insisted that each column should talk about wine, or at least tequila. Over the years I've found hundreds of ways to write about all sorts of things, while somehow linking them to wine. But this rejected column had plenty of wine stuff in it, as well as LSD, intrigue, deception, the Taliban, and all sorts of current interest topics. Did I mention that it was really funny?

Humor, of course, is a very personal thing. Humor is also different from comedy. There are loads of people who write comedy. They sit down and work, rework, and polish their material until it glistens with jocularity. They sell it or perform it or turn it into plays and movies that make us laugh until tears roll down our cheeks. They take their twisted views of our normal world, and slant them with their personal wit until the warped images appear to us wildly misshapen. That's what makes us laugh.

I like comedy, but I have great respect for humor. It's hard to do. For Jake Lorenzo, good humor has to be spontaneous. It comes up in conversation. It's spur of the moment, instantly topical, and hard to remember. Certain things are funny. Sex is funny. Golf is funny. Tennis is not funny. Think about how many jokes you've heard about sex and golf. Now tell me all those tennis jokes. Humor needs to be fearless. There can be no taboos when you're trying to be funny. Stop for a split second to think about the political correctness of a humorous thought, and it's gone, like a fruity zinfandel in the face of a brettanamyces infection.

In today's hustle, bustle, post-9/11 world most people are grumpy, busy, worried, and preoccupied. It's hard to bust 'em on the funny bone, even though a good laugh would make them feel better. People read so little that all sorts of clever references, puns, and similes sail right over their heads. People have become so self important, they can't take a joke, and they spend way too much time worrying about offending someone to ever be funny.

You know what's great about humor. Not everybody laughs at the same stuff. Jake Lorenzo loved Steve Allen, George and Gracie, Groucho, Norm Crosby and Richard Pryor. Bob Hope never cracked me up. W.C. Fields looked *and* talked funny. Buster Keaton was a genius and Charlie Chaplin was the king. The Three Stooges were repetitive. Lenny Bruce, Sam Kinneson, and Chris Rock knew no boundaries, but their visions were often profoundly funny. Tom Green is incredibly gross, but he doesn't make me laugh.

A person with a good sense of humor can make other people laugh at anything, no matter how tragic, no matter how personal, no matter how tasteless the subject. Jake Lorenzo is for laughter. I would rather sit at a table with friends, sip some good wine, and have an evening filled with laughter than anything else in this life. When I look back on all of the friends I have made, I see that the ones I kept have a sense of humor.

You want to laugh? Have Ray Kaufman tell you about losing his passport down an Asian toilet. Get Jim McCullough to talk about any recent trip. Sit and listen to Jerry Henry talk about anything, or try to figure whatever Molly Sessions is trying to tell you. Get Chuy going on one of his rants, or get Iggy Calamari putting spin on one of his failed experiments. That stuff is funny.

Jake will tell you a secret. A great sense of humor requires one to laugh at himself. When you are dealing with humor, sooner or later, it's going to be your turn in the barrel. The time will come when you are the butt of the jokes. Don't ever get upset, or defensive, or mad, because that just makes you a bigger target. My advice: go with the flow. Laugh along, and try to top them by making jokes at your own expense.

Just as a great bottle of wine is made all the better next to a fine meal, humor is much more enjoyable in the presence of great laughers. Jakelyn's mother is a terrific laugher. She cackles with delight at all sorts of things. She giggles on the phone. She busts a funny bone at sitcoms and even commercials. When we're in a New Orleans theater laughing at Ricky Graham and Becky Allen, her laughter rings out with such clarity, that the actors on stage will announce, "She's back."

Last night, at dinner, we were drinking a bottle of Napa Cabernet. "It's a first release from a newly famous vineyard," I told her.

"It's not bad," she said. "Tastes like a lot of other Napa Cabernets pretending to be better than it is."

"They're getting $85.00 per bottle. How's that for pretending?"

And she started to laugh. First with a giggle, then laughing, followed by choking while trying to suppress the laughter. "$85.00," she gasped as tears squeezed out of her eyes. She placed the glass down a little clumsily, spilling a few drops.

"Be careful," I entreated, "you just spilled about four dollars' worth."

She stuck her fingers into the glass and flicked some wine at me. "Here's another two bucks' worth, coming at you."

I dipped my forefinger into the glass, and dabbed it behind my ear. "I don't think you're supposed to drink the stuff, you're meant to wear it."

I guess you had to be there. We had fun. We laughed a bit. We finished the bottle. Dollar for dollar, it certainly wasn't the funniest bottle of wine we've ever shared. No way. You can have plenty of laughs with a $7 Rhone on a spring afternoon with a bunch of winemaking friends. You can laugh your way into the early morning hours with a couple of good bottles of homemade tempranillo if you're drinking with Steve and Lan who don't seem to require sleep on weekends.

Humor is so personal. Now, that I think about it, maybe Practical Winery and Vineyards was kidding me when they rejected that column. The column must have been so perfect that they were requesting no changes, so they decided to tease me instead. It was Jake Lorenzo's turn in the barrel. You think?

TERROR FOR THE TALIBAN

By
Wendell Leibowitz and Lisa Cowen

MAZAR-E-SHARIF, Afghanistan—The freezing cold of Afghan winter covers the surrounding mountains with piles of snow and ice three feet thick rendering dirt roads and mountain trails impassable. The Northern Alliance must wait for spring before advancing on the capital city of Kabul. Yet this nation with no regular electric service, no television, and precious little radio coverage is buzzing with news.

The Americans have put LSD in the tea.

Afghanistan has no healthy water supply. Water flows through the cities in open trenches. The same trenches used for bathing or washing fruits and vegetables are also used as outdoor bathrooms. Boiling water for tea sterilizes the disease bearing microbes often found in Afghan water. Tea is the national beverage. Tea is a national passion full of ritual and portent, and now the tea is laced with LSD.

Confirmed reports from Kabul describe Taliban leaders rounding up Afghan citizens and forcing them to drink tea to see if it is contaminated. One Taliban leader, who spoke under the condition of anonymity, said, "Tea is sacred. Only madmen would seek to adulterate our tea with hallucinogens."

In the United States, government officials refuse to confirm or deny the reports. Dr. Iggy Calamari, inventor of the wine-powered pace maker, and a recently hired consultant to the CIA, spoke at a press conference. "People forget that LSD was originally developed by the United States government as a potential weapon to disorient opposition soldiers. I can't confirm that it has found its way into the Afghan tea supply, but I would imagine an acid trip would certainly expand the consciousness of the Taliban."

Pentagon spokesmen also refuse to confirm or deny reports about LSD in the tea, but they take every opportunity to remind reporters that this terrorist war is unlike any other war we've fought, and that it requires new methods of combat. They vociferously deny, however, that thousands of old eight-track Grateful Dead tapes are being dropped along with food aid into Afghanistan.

As if LSD laced tea is not enough to strike terror into the heart of the Taliban, new rumors blossoming from Peshawar, Pakistan describe hundreds of thousands of bottles of chardonnay being smuggled into Afghanistan and distributed to the people. The wine is in plastic containers with screw caps. The wine is purported to be from the 2001 vintage from California. It is made in a crisp, high-acid Chablis style with no malolactic fermentation and very little oak aging.

A shadowy figure named Jake Lorenzo is thought to be connected with the wine invasion. Our research shows that Mr. Lorenzo helped Abbie Hoffman organize a demonstration in the 60's where demonstrators attempted to levitate the Pentagon. At the time, there were widespread reports that LSD had been added to the water supply. Government records also show that Mr. Lorenzo spent time in Afghanistan with a daughter named Jakelyn and a woman believed to be his wife. The threesome entered Afghanistan in December of 1975 and left in March of 1976. Records also show them in Pakistan, Iran, and Turkey. More recently, Mr. Lorenzo has worked as a private investigator in the town of Sonoma, California.

Jesus "Chuy" Palacios, owner of Chuy's Burrito Palace and reportedly a good friend of Mr. Lorenzo said, "I don't know where Jake is, and I wouldn't tell you if I did. I know that he doesn't like chardonnay, so I wouldn't put it past him. I mean it would be like killing three birds with one bottle. Jake gets rid of a bunch of chardonnay, makes a lot of Afghans happy in dreary times, and pisses off the fundamentalist Taliban."

A spokesman for the California wine industry was incensed. "Chardonnay from California is some of the best wine in the world. That anyone would put it in plastic bottles with screw caps is an abomination. We are considering legal action."

Chardonnay prices have dropped precipitously in 2001 as a glut of the grape overwhelmed sluggish sales. Several winemakers in Sonoma talked of "giving chardonnay grapes to anyone who would take the things away." Many of these same winemakers admit to knowing Jake Lorenzo, but none of them will confirm actually giving him any chardonnay grapes. Weight tags from the grapes have mysteriously disappeared, and government officials from the BATF refuse to answer our calls.

Chuy Palacios had a unique take on events, "LSD in the tea and free California chardonnay, Afghanistan may become *the* hot tourist destination next season."

MOVING ON

Chuy speaks quietly to the esteemed Dr. Iggy Calamari, inventor of the wine-powered pacemaker. Dr. Calamari nods occasionally as he shovels forkful after forkful of Chuy's chorizo and eggs into his mouth.

"I'm telling you, Dr. Iggy, something is wrong with Señor Jake. He's got no fire. He is too much *tranquilo*. I am very worried."

Dr. Calamari emits a gentle belch. "Chuy, no one makes chorizo and eggs like you, and the little slab of chilaquiles on the side is pure heaven."

"What, are you loco, Dr. Iggy? I'm telling you that our friend Señor Jake is in big troubles, and you compliment my sausage, what kind of help is that?"

"Relax Chuy, I will look into the matter. In fact, if I am not mistaken, the great Mr. Lorenzo approaches as we speak."

Jake Lorenzo, private eye walks into the Burrito Palace with a comfortable familiarity. He ambles to the counter and sits on a stool, his stool, *"la silla de Jake."*

"How's it hanging, Iggy?" Turning to Chuy, Jake says, *"Buenas días*, Chuy, I could use a cup of coffee and don't be light with the tequila."

Chuy pours a cup of coffee, adds a generous portion of tequila, and disappears into the kitchen to let the good doctor make his analysis. Dr. Calamari and Jake hold an animated conversation, as Jake works his way through his own platter of chorizo and eggs. When Jake goes to the phone to check his messages, Chuy scurries to the counter.

"What do you think, Dr. Iggy? Is it something serious?"

"He seems perfectly normal to me, Chuy. We talked for twenty minutes. He still seems the sarcastic, pensive private detective we've all come to love and appreciate."

"You must be blinds," protests Chuy. "Here he comes, watch this."

Jake sits down, as Chuy refills his coffee cup, and pours in another shot of tequila. "Yo, Jake. I just been reading that Arrowood released his new merlot. He got a 94 in the *Wine Enthusiast*, and it's selling for $48 a bottle."

Jake sips his coffee. "Yeah, old Mike Berthoud and Dick have been making some pretty good merlot for a lot of years. Hey, Iggy, you know anything about dahlias? A friend just gave me a bunch of bulbs."

Before Iggy can say anything, Chuy blurts out, "Hey Jake, did you see that the new Turley wines are out already? 1995 zins and petite sirahs in that $35-$45 per bottle range."

"No kidding," says Jake, "Iggy, did you know that Larry Turley was an emergency room doctor? You guys probably have a lot in common." Jake stands up, and slaps Iggy on the back. "I've got to go, Doc. I'll be spending the day in the archives looking at land transactions for a client. Stop by for a glass of wine this evening, if you've got the time."

"You see, Dr. Iggy. I told you something is wrong with Señor Jake. He always goes crazy with high wine prices, no matter how good the wine is. You know how he screams about wine scores. And wine magazines, I don't got to tell you. So I feed him this information, and what do we get? We get dahlia bulbs, that's what. I'm telling you, something's wrong, *mucho* wrong."

Dr. Calamari, pulls at his chin. "Perhaps, you are onto something, my good friend, and since I have an invitation to drink some of Jake's wine this evening, I assure you I will follow up on your concerns."

That night, as Iggy and I sip our way through a few bottles of pinot noir with Jakelyn's mother, he tells me about Chuy's concerns. "The guy is really worried, Jake, and I've got to admit, you would have made some comment about those wines in the past. What gives?"

Jake Lorenzo sits for a minute, quietly sipping at his $12 Benton Lane pinot noir. "Well, Iggy, there's no sense in beating a dead horse, and Jake Lorenzo is no whiner."

We pulled the stuffed quail off the barbecue. Jakelyn's mother finished up the port sauce, and we had a delicious, simple dinner with a $10 bottle of Noceto sangiovese. We talked about all kinds of things. When Dr. Iggy Calamari got in the cab to go home, he was full, a bit tipsy, and convinced that Jake Lorenzo was just fine.

You see, the bottom line is that Jake Lorenzo loves wine. I like the whole concept of it. I love the connection to nature and the annual phoenix-like rebirth of the vines. I can't wait for the vines to leaf out, then flower, and then set their fruit. Veraision should be a holiday. Crush is pure adrenaline. Tasting young wines, is like starting on a new case, looking for clues, and guessing where they will take you. And as for drinking— sitting at a table with fine food, friends, and a few bottles is all Jake Lorenzo asks of life.

Jake Lorenzo has no problems with wine. The wine business, on the other hand is a different thing. To be perfectly honest, Jake Lorenzo is bored. I am bored by the hype, by the stories, by the auctions, and by the same old, same old. I can't get it up to rant and rave about wine prices anymore.

I believe I have matured to a new level. I enjoy wine. I appreciate wine. I make wine a daily part of my life and my meals, but I no longer follow reviews, or press releases. I have three different wine purveyors who know what I like, and what I can afford. I rely upon them to suggest wines, and I support them with my dollars. Lately, it means that Jake Lorenzo is drinking Cotes du Rhone, Australian shiraz, the occasional Chilean. If one searches, there are still finds in California, Oregon and Washington.

Dining in restaurants can present a problem, so I try to partake in restaurants at lunch-time, where an inexpensive sauvignon blanc or riesling is much more appropriate. Faced with a typical wine list, I search for a bargain, and finding none, I have gone back to ordering a beer.

Wine will always remain a passion for Jake Lorenzo, but now I treat it like any other of the earth's great bounties. Wine has become a mainstay of my life, and my meals. I know a good one when it is in my glass. My budget restricts my choices, but not enough to diminish my ability to drink quality. My appreciation of wine is no different than my appreciation of sweet, ripe garden fresh tomatoes, or a succulent farm raised piece of lamb. The difference is that, with all its other magical properties, wine makes Jake Lorenzo high, and I like that too, especially while I'm waiting for my dahlias to bloom.

GIMME A JAKE

Jake Lorenzo needs help. In Oliver's, the great downtown bar at the Mayflower Park Hotel in Seattle, he's getting it. Jake is in Oliver's for a book signing. Copies of *Cold Surveillance* are displayed prominently and artistically amongst bottles of tequila and the free hors d'oeuvres.

Marc Nowak, hotel General Manager, has high expectations. After all, it's Friday night, and Jake has just killed them on KIRO's Noon News program, not to mention the Larry Nelson show on KOMO radio.

Jake knows better. More than 200 people are packed into the bar, smoking up a storm and downing Oliver's deservedly famous martinis. They could care less about Jake Lorenzo. The room's ambiance shouts, "We're here to drink, not to read."

This is fine with Jake. I'm ensconced at a choice corner seat at the bar trying to invent a drink. The bartenders, Patrick, Michael and Steve, are helping, while they pump out hundreds of cocktails for the thirsty crowd.

On a recent trip to Mexico, where I was doing research for my new book on tequila, I was reading an old John MacDonald novel featuring Travis McGee. In this novel, Travis and his friends were drinking cocktails named after the hero. I figured what's good enough for Travis McGee is good enough for Jake Lorenzo. The McGee featured gin. My drink will have to feature tequila, of course.

Inventing a cocktail isn't easy. For starters, Patrick made a Jake's Inspiration. This is the martini they named after me as their entry into the 1994 martini competition. It's a Bombay Sapphire Gin martini that uses prickly pear-infused Patron tequila in place of vermouth—very nice.

Then Michael mixed an Oliver's martini, named Seattle's finest classic martini for five straight years—extraordinary. Then we got down to work. We used lime rubs, liquor rinses, heavy shakers, major strainers and after hours of serious tastings we had the world's first tequila martini, simply named "The Jake."

Here's how it's done. Take a long strip of lime zest and rub the inside of a chilled pint glass. Pour 1 ounce of good cabernet or syrah into the pint glass and rinse the inside. Discard the wine. Fill the glass with ice. Pour in 1½ ounces of Hornitos tequila. (Any one of your favorite 100% agave tequilas will work so long as they are *blancos*.) Cover the glass with a metal shaker, and shake like hell while whistling the bridge to *Tequila* by the Champs. Let rest for one minute, then strain into a chilled martini glass. Garnish with a long curled strip of lime zest.

The finished drink should have tiny ice crystals floating on top. It should be brilliantly clear with a delicate pink hue. The first sip will have the slightest rough edge to it, and subsequent sips will get smoother and smoother. The second Jake will relax all major muscle groups. A third Jake will dissolve all vestiges of mental or physical stress. More than three Jakes are the cocktailing equivalent of electric shock therapy and can lead to temporary loss of memory and/or consciousness.

You know, Jake Lorenzo has been writing about wine for more than 12 years. I'm the author of the very successful *Cold Surveillance*, which tells about life in the wine country in a very humorous way. In all those 12 years of writing about wine, I've received a total of three bottles of wine in the mail. That's it. Figuring a six-ounce pour, that works out to a little more than one glass per year. Believe me, Jake Lorenzo needs more than that to brush his teeth, let alone keep abreast of current wine trends.

Now, I'm simply *talking* about writing a book on tequila. I've made one ten-day trip to Mexico to research the project. I've already received 28 bottles of tequila from great producers like Herradura, Sauza, El Tesoro, Porfidio and Centinela. Tequila guys are looking for people to try their products and write about them. They are eager and pleased to offer their products for sampling, and I plan on rewarding them for their generosity.

As long as my liver will hold out, I've embarked on the largest tasting of tequila ever carried out in this country. I've enlisted some great sensory analysts, and we hope to develop descriptors for the various tequilas so consumers will have some idea of the different styles available.

We will not be rating them on some ridiculous 100-point scale. We will not be hitting them up for ads in some fancy tequila magazine. We will not rag on them about the different ways they make, blend and age their products. We're simply tasting more than 300 tequilas and reporting on our impressions, because it seems like a fun thing to do.

The tequila industry will benefit, because a funny, informative, informal book will be published about their product. Jake Lorenzo and my friends will have a great time tasting all kinds of tequilas and pounding down Jakes. Hopefully, I will learn all there is to know about tequila, its production, its flavors and its effects upon the central nervous system. If things work out, Jake Lorenzo could be Mr. Tequila in America.

When are you wine guys going to figure it out? Stop sending all those wine samples to Robert Parker, *The Wine Spectator*, and the *Wine Enthusiast*. Anthony Blue, Bob Thompson, Hugh Johnson and their counterparts receive so many samples of wine that they probably pay a service to haul them away.

Wise up. Send those samples to Jake Lorenzo. I won't rate them. You won't get some score based on a 100-point system. You won't read some sublime description of the subtle flavors bursting from your bottle. You also won't get some call hitting you up for a half-page ad. You won't be asked to kick in $600 for a table so you can pour your wines at my charity event.

Send the samples. I'll drink them with my friends. If we like them, I'll write you a card telling you so. What could be better than that? I'll tell you what. Take this column to your favorite bar. Have the bartender make you a couple of Jakes. When you regain consciousness, give my proposal some thought.

Let's see what turns up in the mail.

PART II

FAMILY, HOME AND HEARTH

Weddings

Grandpa Jake

Environmental Factors

More Than a Home

Construction

Hard Times

Hunting

Labor Day

Grapevines and Grandbabies

Dad

WEDDINGS

All parents think that their children are special, well-adjusted and well-meaning. Parents believe this to be true, no matter how weird, wild or rebellious their children's behavior. With Jake Lorenzo's daughter, however, we definitely have that rarest of all children; a truly special, well-adjusted and well-meaning child...ask anyone.

My daughter, Jakelyn Lorenzo, was married last week.

Marriage remains one of the truly mythical, mystical rites in our jaded modern society. It is loaded with meaningful moments from the walk down the aisle, to the vows, to the first dance. The time leading up to a marriage, especially the week preceding the actual nuptials, is one of unequaled tension and stress.

Jake Lorenzo knows this to be true, because on more than one occasion I had to coax Jakelyn's mother down from the ceiling, after she had gone off like a rocket over some insignificant point of contention.

Jakelyn, on the other hand, was the picture of focused good cheer. Jakelyn, who as a child did not strike me as overly sentimental, did have this habit of buying wedding books and planning her wedding as soon as a boy asked her out on the first date. Fortunately, for old Jake, she grew up in a house full of brutally funny sarcasm. No one was spared, and Jakelyn, in self-defense, developed a sarcastic, quick wit that she unleashed upon her teenage suitors whenever they behaved in some typically adolescent manner.

Teenage boys may be a lot of things, but they are certainly not ready to take inventive, hilarious tongue-lashings from their young dates. Jakelyn rarely went on second dates despite being the cute, vivacious cheerleader that she was.

For her wedding, Jakelyn had planned things down to the last detail. There were to be eight children in the wedding, six of them under five. Twelve adults would march down the aisle in front of her. The boy children wore matching vests and shorts, sewn by Jakelyn. The girl children and all the bridesmaids wore dresses, sewn by Jakelyn. The groomsmen, fathers, and groom all wore matching ties, sewn, of course, by Jakelyn.

Calm as her outward appearance, Jakelyn evidently suffered some stress of her own. For weeks before the wedding, she fought a persistent bronchitis, which sapped her strength and caused her to lose 10 pounds, weight she could ill afford to be without. This weight loss led to the incident that I most remember.

Three days before the wedding, I sat on the porch with my daughter, who calmly spooned birdseed into satin roses (sewn by Jakelyn). Inside the house, Jakelyn's mom, aunt Vivian and cousin Maya had ripped the handmade wedding gown into four separate pieces and were trying to put it back together so it would accommodate her weight loss. Jakelyn conversed with dear old dad, poured birdseed into the satin roses, (and all over the damn porch,) and calmly went into the house every fifteen minutes for yet another fitting. It was a stunning display of courage.

She had decided to have the wedding performed at Gundlach Bundschu Winery. Lance Cutler performed the nuptials. The kids cast rose petals. The food, music and flavor was decidedly Cajun, reflecting her schooling at Loyola in New Orleans. Over 300 of our good friends from across the country attended.

Jakelyn was the beautiful bride. Her groom was left speechless, watching as she walked down the aisle. Even hard-bitten Jake Lorenzo, private eye, had a catch in his throat and some mist around the eyes.

The party, after the ceremony, was terrific. Chuy Palacios catered. The hit of the evening was either the Mexican-flavored Cajun fried turkey, or the six foot by three foot wedding cake laden with twenty pounds of fresh berries.

The defining moment of the event came as I stood in the food line, behind the bride and groom. Jakelyn had stopped, and was talking to the girl serving the Cajun fried turkey. Behind her stood her husband, Robbie. The young man serving the salad gazed down on Jakelyn's breasts as he absent-mindedly piled more and more salad on Robbie's plate. Finally, Robbie nudged Jakelyn and said, "Let's get a move on, my plate won't hold any more salad."

Jake Lorenzo had to smile. I hadn't lost a daughter. I had gained a son.

*   *   *

Later, basking in the after-glow of the wedding, and enjoying the peace and quiet of a finally empty house, Jake Lorenzo sits thinking about vineyards. Vineyards are like children in that every farmer thinks his vineyard is special, producing the finest produce, capable of making the best wine. Wine makers know that grapes are the raw product from which they work their magic, and they remain confident of their abilities to work with these grapes to make fabulous wines.

Jake Lorenzo drinks wine every day, usually more than one bottle. It seems to me that since 1987 most wines are thinner than they used to be. There's generally less tannic backbone, and less intensity of fruit. Wines are all starting to taste the same.

Wine writers blame this phenomenon on shared information in the industry. They imagine wine makers, all trained at Fresno or Davis, copying the same techniques to achieve roughly the same results. Fining methods and especially filtration regimens are named as culprits. I think this is ridiculous.

Grapes are the source material from which wines are made. The reason wine makers are so free with their methods, is that they know duplicating the methods cannot overcome the unique character of the individual vineyards. "You can copy my methods, but my wines will still be different, because they come from different grapes."

Yet, I must agree, wines are starting to taste more and more alike. When I attend one of those gigantic tastings where over 100 wines are being poured, I rarely find anything that pops out as terrific. Nowadays, it's all I can do to find a couple that will entice me to have a second glass. Granted, 1988 and 1989 weren't great vintages, but this mediocre uniformity is starting to show in the 1990's, a supposedly great vintage.

Jake Lorenzo says forget the wine makers. Stop talking about filtration and fining. Go back to the vineyard.

Ten to fifteen years ago, wines may have lacked finesse, but they were loaded with character. Crops were kept small, around three tons to the acre. Most vineyards were dry-farmed, or used a single deep soak irrigation from the overhead sprinklers.

Now, everyone has drip irrigation. Put the water to the vines. Manage the canopy. Increase the yield. Trellis. Strip the leaves. What a crock.

Jake Lorenzo would like to suggest that drip irrigation is slowly ruining the character of California's wines. If you think California wines are losing their character and their intensity, if you think the wines are all tasting alike, then look for the cure in the vineyard, not the winery.

Farmers, do me a favor. Sit down with your wine makers and taste the wines made from your produce. Taste those wines back to the late 70's. Allow for the vagaries of vintage and aging, but truthfully evaluate the character of those wines. If you see a loss of intensity, and I think you will, coincide that loss with when you put in your drip system. Is there a correlation? I bet there is.

Be honest. The future of your industry is at stake. If I'm right, correcting the problem is simple. Figure out better ways to manage your irrigation systems. Devise them to produce character and intensity instead of textbook numbers and increased yields.

Jake Lorenzo knows it's a radical notion. Think about it. Consider it a wedding present.

GRANDPA JAKE

Jake Lorenzo's a Grandpa. Actually, I've been a Grandpa for two years. So far, I've been doing a pretty good job at it, although I don't get to spend much time with the grandbaby. Jakelyn's mother spends a lot more time with her than I do. It seems that every time Jake Lorenzo has a case that takes him out of Sonoma, Grandma is on a plane to see Jakelyn and the grandbaby.

The grandbaby just had her second birthday, and is talking up a storm, although she speaks in a special language that only her mother and father fully comprehend. Jake Lorenzo is not thrilled to see the grandbaby speaking. Already my monthly phone bills have escalated to the point that AT&T sends me monthly checks thanking me for my patronage. Yesterday, Candace Bergen stopped by the house to make a personal plea for me to change long distance companies. How much higher can Jake Lorenzo's phone bill go once Jakelyn's mother starts giving advice and conversation to the grand baby?

Jakelyn, the grandbaby, the grandpuppy and the son-in-law came down for a visit last month. The grandbaby is charming. She runs around like the Energizer Bunny, going and going and going, and it's not until Jakelyn forcibly removes the batteries (puts her down) that the poor child actually rests. Grandpa took her out to Laura Chenel's to play with the goats, although at this point in time, the grandbaby is not fond of chevre. She is fond of most other foodstuffs, and resembles nothing so much as a garbage disposal, swallowing whatever she shoves into her aperture, and requiring Jakelyn to occasionally remove the odd spoon or rock or bug.

Grandparents love their grandchildren. Jake Lorenzo is no exception. I've heard other grandparents say the reason they love their grandchildren is, "They go home." That's not it at all. Grandchildren are delightful, because they force the realization of generation. I love watching my daughter and son-in-law deal with the grandbaby. Everything that baby does is, more or less, something that Jakelyn did. In watching them, I am reminded of me and Jakelyn's mom raising Jakelyn. Those are happy memories.

I am also reminded that I am a Grandpa. Another generation removed from the life source. It matters not that all of us are living longer. It matters not that we are healthier and more fit for our age than anyone else has ever been. Grandchildren and great grandchildren for that matter define our place in the succession of life. They remind us that we are older, and they demand that we use our experience to act wisely.

Somehow, this generational reminder provided by my grandbaby got Jake Lorenzo thinking about the California wine business. The California wine business, you see, is still in its first generation, and what a generation it is. The whole industry is based, not on being handed down from one generation to another, but from a complete rejection of those values. Most California winery owners rejected earlier business lives. They left the family business, or the jobs for which they were trained, to seek out a new, more rural life. They devised a unique industry based on their simple love for the product. Even the great Robert Mondavi started the California premium wine business by splitting from his traditional family business and striking out after his own vision.

A second wave of producers came into the wine business, not through succession, but by choice. People successful at other careers took a look at the burgeoning wine industry, and charmed by the romance of it, decided to try their hand at it. Stockbrokers, building contractors, lawyers and movie directors for reasons close to their hearts moved into the wine business, but they too were moved by a love for the product.

Now, 30 years after the initial boom that led to the premium California wine business, a second generation is poised to take over. The sons and daughters of the visionaries who built a multi-million dollar industry based on the love of wine and the wine life are about to take over the reins. What is their vision? Where will they take us in the next 20 years?

I'll tell you the truth; this whole thing makes Jake Lorenzo a little bit nervous. Because America is a country born of revolution, and because we are a society based on individualism, we often expect our kids to make their own way. We may want them to continue the family business, but it's their choice. If they want to do something else, we'll understand. That's as it should be, especially in America. Unfortunately, this attitude causes us to pass up important training opportunities.

If we look to Europe, we'll see wine families that have gone on for hundreds of years, passing from one generation to the next. Europeans have a history of succession, and they train their children for it. European wine families have their children work in the wineries. They learn, first hand, how to make wine, to clean tanks, to lug hoses, and to stand for long hours on the bottling line. They are sent to the fields to prune vines, pick grapes and drive tractors. As they get older they are sent to foreign countries to study different winemaking techniques and to learn other languages.

Finally, when they are ready to get involved in the business, they are given small tasks, which ensure success. Perhaps they are given one city in which to market their wines. Maybe they are given one block of grapes to plant and care for. Perhaps they are put in charge of a single lot of wine. Little by little, they take on responsibility, meet success, and then take on more responsibility. Eventually, after years of preparation they are ready to take over, and the company is assured of a continuation of family business values.

It ain't like that here.

In America, we tend not to train our children. We forget how much training and how many years of experience went into building our own expertise. We have not the talent for devising situations in which our children are both challenged, yet assured success. In Europe, they invest time and gently nurture the future generation, much the way we nurture a grapevine. The American training program is "Sink or swim."

Jake Lorenzo thinks that there is too much at stake for us to continue this particular American tradition in this particular case. Wine is too magical a product. The wine life is too precious a commodity. The appreciation of wine and the life it affords us is too special a gift for us to risk our children rejecting it.

It is the job of every parent to strive for a better life for his or her children. There is no better gift we can bestow on our children than the appreciation of working hard at something they love to make a product that brings pleasure to so many. It is our responsibility to take the time and care required to guarantee the proper passage of our passion for wine. We must not blame our children, if we are the ones too entrenched to change our attitudes for their betterment.

Who knows, maybe if we can learn to do this for our children, then their children will live in a better world. They might even think their grandparents were pretty cool, even if they drank a hell of a lot.

ENVIRONMENTAL FACTORS

The grand-baby called Jake Lorenzo for Father's Day.

"Happy Father's Day, Paw Paw," she said. Clear as a bell.

Grandchildren amaze Jake Lorenzo, especially mine. Jakelyn expected to wait a little longer in her marriage before having her first child. To that end she bought a dog, a beagle don't you know. Beagles are great dogs, especially if you are the daughter of a private eye.

Beagles do two things. They hunt, and they eat, much like private eyes.

Jakelyn raised their beagle to live inside. That means the dog doesn't hunt. All she does is eat. Beagles are powerful, and they are determined. You don't want to get between Jakelyn's beagle and its food.

Now, the grandbaby grew up thinking that Desiree (the beagle) was her sister. They played together, fought over snacks, and played tug of war with each other's toys. All siblings go through this, but few children have beagles for siblings.

Desiree is tough. Grab a towel and let her bite onto the other end of it, and you can lift her clear off the ground, because she isn't about to let go. Take her for a walk, and even a man of Jake Lorenzo's strength is likely to be dragged along to where she is headed. Grow up with Desiree, and you are stronger than people imagine.

The grandbaby is a cute kid. On the outside, she looks like most other kids. She's not tall or particularly big, but she is some strong. Pushing and pulling against Desiree, the beagle, for her entire life has built up some muscles. When she interacts with other kids, and things come to a push or a shove, the other kids go flying. This show of strength is surprising in a petite three-year old. Day care workers assess this phenomenon by saying, "She needs to work on her sharing skills."

When the grandbaby has had a rough day, and really needs to work on her sharing skills, Jakelyn takes away her computer time.

You see, Jake's son-in-law is a computer whiz kid. Among other things he designs computer programs that allow the computers to talk to their printers. His house is loaded with computers, CD-ROMS, printers, and all kinds of high tech equipment, that Jake Lorenzo wouldn't even know how to turn on. The grandbaby, on the other hand, has learned all kinds of computer stuff, and she is righteously pissed off when her computer time is denied.

I guess Jake Lorenzo would feel the same way if Jakelyn's mother wouldn't let me drink pinot noir with my meals. The point of all this revolves around the effects of environment upon our individual personalities.

Last week Jakelyn's mother and I dined at Babette's here in Sonoma. Fantastic is too weak a descriptor for the food put out by Chef Daniel Patterson. Supremely dedicated to cooking, Chef Daniel oversees every detail from procuring the raw product, to preparing it, and presenting the final dish. The meal begins with some tiny morsel; perhaps a perfectly prepared half quail egg, with the tiniest dollop of a spectacular sauce, topped with a bit of caviar.

For a first course, Chef Daniel has devised a chive flan, topped with beluga caviar, served inside an alabaster white eggshell perched on a gleaming stainless steel egg cup. Jake Lorenzo wonders how you even attempt to cut off the top of an egg shell, and then I ponder how many eggs I would break before I got it right.

Next, a perfectly cooked slice of foie gras sits in a pretty dribble of dark brown sauce, decorated with poached, pitted, delicately ripened Bing cherries.

Each dish is intensely delicious, sublimely complex, and sized so that your appetite hungers for the next course. Which, in this case, turns out to be lamb, crusted on the outside with a melody of herbs, succulent with its medium rare juices, set off with baby Yukon gold potatoes, and tiny carrots woven into a braid by their brilliant green tops.

A choice selection of cheese follows the main course. Each cheese perfectly ripened, and arranged on bright green watercress, or delicately spindled escarole, with the barest hint of olive oil or balsamic vinegar.

Desserts are gorgeous, festive, and intense without ever tasting sweet. Coffee is rich, dark. Service is attentive and formal. The wines are reasonably priced and eccentric enough to interest.

After dinner, Daniel sits with us to have a glass of wine. Jake Lorenzo gazes at this culinary master. He is six months younger than Jakelyn. What kind of environment did Daniel come from that made him so dedicated to cooking and fine dining? How does so young a man, determine to challenge himself in so classic a manner?

The point of this description is that even private eyes are affected by environment.

Jake Lorenzo has a prejudice. I prefer things to be small, owned and operated by individuals who pursue their own visions. Chuy's Burrito Palace, while completely different from Babette's, is no less unique and delicious.

When I started to drink wine, wineries were tiny. Individuals worked alone, or with one or two friends to chase their visions. Jake Lorenzo spends a lot of time searching for tiny, individual operations. I want to buy a bottle of wine, and then be able to walk up to the person who made it and shake their hand. I want a single person to be responsible, good or bad. I prefer winemakers who do the work themselves, in small amounts, to please their own sensibilities.

Jake Lorenzo doesn't believe that small wineries, operated by winemakers, make better wines than large wineries with huge crews, and pages of work orders, and whole marketing departments. I do like to believe that if I support these tiny, dedicated artistic ventures, they may succeed and show us a better way.

I've got to go. Jakelyn's on the phone. Evidently the grandbaby has just entered the room with a print of her latest computer drawing. Since neither Jakelyn, nor her husband had turned the printer on for the grandbaby, some investigation may be necessary.

MORE THAN A HOME

Wanderlust defined me. Travel was my narcotic. As soon as the bank account reached $1,000, Jake Lorenzo started looking for cheap tickets. I would pack up my daughter Jakelyn and her mother at a moment's notice, and we'd be off to Afghanistan or Greece or someplace else in Europe. Once, when a friend loaned me a camper, we took off for three months around the United States. If Jakelyn's mom wanted a margarita, we were likely to spend the next few weeks in Mexico on some beach.

Before Jake knew it, Los Angeles was a series of apartments between trips. It certainly wasn't home. Jakelyn was seven years old, and we had moved nine times. We made the move to Sonoma in 1977, having rented a small, two-bedroom, 864-square-foot house just outside town.

I'll never forget Jakelyn's squeal of delight when we drove up in the U-Haul and deer came bounding across the street in front of our house. We pulled into our driveway around 1 a.m., walked into the house, and went to sleep on the floor covering ourselves with moving tarps. The next morning, we were awakened by donkeys braying, a sound like laughter at a good joke. Jake Lorenzo knew he was home.

Twenty-three years later, we live in that same house, still renting. A lot has happened in that house. One of the reasons Jakelyn's mom and I have gotten along is that she enjoys guests as much as I do. Sure, it took her a while to get used to Jake Lorenzo bringing groups of unannounced strangers to dinner, but once she explained to me that I'd be doing all of the cooking, we were fine.

That little house in Sonoma turned into an honest-to-goodness home. Jakelyn grew up, and the memories are many. She still won't forgive Jake Lorenzo for wearing a bright red dashiki to her junior high school graduation. Later, I remember her sitting on the porch, filling homemade satin flowers with birdseed for her wedding, while her mom and aunt frantically sewed her wedding gown together. Then there was the first visit of the grandbaby, and the time the grandpuppy crapped on the carpet.

The house was special for so many people besides us. Scores of visitors drank at our trough of plenty, replenishing their souls with good times and fine food, nourishing themselves with a sense of family. The list of people who have fed their souls at this little house boggles the mind, and the events we have contrived will never occur again.

Oswald Lehnart, the classical violinist for the Pablo Casal's Trio played a private one-man concert for 24 invited guests on our porch. Every time he put bow to fiddle, my landlord's dog would howl. After Joe Torre had been fired as manager of the St. Louis Cardinals, and before the New York Yankees hired him, he spent an afternoon in our garage with his wife Ali bottling our homemade wine. Len Cariou, Tony award-winning Broadway actor, performed 20 minutes of Dracula shtick wearing the cape I used to hijack the Napa Wine Train. Charmaine Neville and her band didn't wake up for picking grapes, but they managed to get to the house in time to press out a load, and then eat a California crawfish boil done with lobsters.

This house has hosted some of the finest winemakers in California and from around the world. Bob Sessions, Dick Arrowood, Helen Turley, Mark Stupich, and Charlie Tolbert. Winemakers from Lafite, Latour, Romanee Conti, and Castello di Rampolla. We've had Benzigers, Sebastianis, Mondavis, and for ten years Bundschus ate here so often, Jake Lorenzo thought they were family.

Every barrel maker from Jean Francois to Alan Fouquet and Mel Knox has been here. We even let wine writers sit at our table, but only the ones who talk about stuff other than wine. People like Gerald Asher, Hugh Johnson, Bob Thompson, Larry Walker, Brian St. Pierre and Rod Smith.

The meals go on and on. Chefs loved to come here for dinner. Not just Sonoma chefs like Keith Filipello, Max Sasser, Manny Alvarado, John McReynolds, and Daniel Patterson, but almost every New Orleans chef who's ever been to California.

We sourced our seafood from Seattle. Bruce Campbell personally delivered his wonderful CK Lamb. We used Rocky Free-Range Chicken, Sonoma Foie Gras, and Hog Island Oysters. We raised our own vegetables, rabbits, and quail. Jakelyn's mom even baked our bread. Our standard dinner toast was, "Food so good that you'll never forget, with enough wine to make it hard to remember."

For every chef or winemaker or baseball player, we had 20 non-celebrity friends. Friends who came on the spur of the moment whenever we scored a load of lobsters or crawfish, or when one of the guys bagged a deer. Duck hunters, abalone divers, and fisherman all delivered their treasures in exchange for nights at our table. They would stop by any time day or night, and corks would be pulled and food would be served.

People would drink themselves out of driving, and then spend the night. The tiny house would turn into a giant futon for friends. Jake Lorenzo provided Tequila Sunrise Services, brunch, lunch, comida, dinner, midnight snacks, and early morning breakfasts. There was food and wine and tequila, and there was always music. More than anything it was friends and family. More than anything, it was life.

We had a great life, and we lived it in that little rental house for 23 years. Now, my landlord has put the house up for sale, and we will have to move. Jake Lorenzo has been priced out of the Sonoma housing market, so I'm not sure where we'll land. But I want to thank all of you who shared our table, enjoyed our home, and helped make our life.

Today I worked in the wine cellar packing bottles. Claude Berthoud dropped by, so we went upstairs and opened a pinot noir. While we were drinking, a couple of friends stopped by with a stripped bass they had caught. We opened some more wine and started cooking. It was a big bass, so I called some more friends to join us for dinner. We went late into the night. I didn't get much packing done, but it occurred to me that a house is not a home except for the people who inhabit it. Our house will change. Jake Lorenzo plans to stay the same.

Sonoma has enough houses. We could use more homes. Maybe if more people poked their heads up from their green screens and their cell phones and their 12-hour workdays, they could turn their houses into homes. They could cook, have dinner with friends, and drink a few bottles of wine. If this strikes you as a good idea, give us a call. Jakelyn's mom and I won't be settled down anywhere for a while, and we're always looking for a good meal with friends.

CONSTRUCTION "What do you
mean, he picks up nails?" asked Dr. Iggy Calamari, inventor of the wine-powered pacemaker.

"I'm telling you," answered Chuy, "every time I visit the building site, Jake is picking up nails."

"Look, Chuy, I've been to that site dozens of times. I've seen Jake digging ditches, I've seen him setting forms, pouring cement, framing, sheathing, and roofing. The guy is building his house at record pace."

Chuy nodded in agreement, "I know, Dr. Iggy, I know, but he's always picking up nails. Why is he always picking up the nails?"

*　　　　　*　　　　　*

Jake Lorenzo is building a house. Notified that his landlord of 23 years had decided to sell his home, Jake had no choice. Sure the house he and Jakelyn's mom had called home for all of those years exuded charm. Their simple kitchen yielded some of the finest meals in wine country. Their legendary porch was recognized as the most delightful drinking spot in all of Sonoma Valley. The two acres surrounding the house displayed a wonderful combination of unspoiled nature and domesticated fruit and vegetable production. But the bottom line revealed that the house was just 846 square feet, and there was no way to justify the $395,000 asking price, even at today's inflated market prices.

So Jake talked to contractors. He talked to sub-contractors. He talked to architects, electricians, carpenters, and plumbers. Quotes were delivered, all at outlandish prices. "Of course, those prices would cover the job," they would say, "if we could get to it, which we can't, because we're so busy making so much money for all of those people paying us these exorbitant prices for our work, when we are able to do it."

Jake calculated. He computed. He sorted through the bids. Jake shook his head sadly. He told Jakelyn's mom. "There's no way we can hire a contractor, or even sub-contractors to build the house. Using their bids, the cheapest we could get away with would be $190–$240 per square foot. We just don't have the money."

"So," asked Jakelyn's mom, "what are we going to do?"

"We'll take that funky shack we bought in Fetters Hot Springs to use as your studio, demo it, and build a new house ourselves," replied Jake. "It's the only way we can afford to stay in the valley."

"Do you know anything about construction?"

"No," said Jake.

"You can do it," Jakelyn's mom encouraged. "Just remember I want a soaking tub and a big picture window in the master bath, and my looms have to fit in the house."

"All of them," asked Jake.

Jakelyn's mother just smiled.

Jake designed the house, had drawings made, and passed them through the county in 42 days. The old wooden house without any foundation that sat on the property disappeared in 48 hours. The three sixty-foot trees infected with beetles were cut, split, and distributed to friends before the first weekend. The house was laid out the same day as the Sonoma Valley Wine Auction. Jake hired three men off the corner, and the four of them hand-dug the foundation in two days. Jake and his part-time carpenters constructed the forms with brand new 2x8s, and then used them as joists in the sub-floor.

"You don't see that much, anymore," said the inspector. "It looks great, and you'll have a sturdy floor that doesn't creak."

Jake and three carpenter friends framed the house in three days. The shear walls went up in two. Trusses were landed, and the roof was nailed in four. Contractors kept stopping by to see the job. "Who's running the job for you?" they would ask.

Jake would smile, "Local guy. He's in and out."

"Have him call me," they would say. "I might have work for him."

Jake paid every bill within 48 hours of receiving it. Each and every person who worked on the house got wine or a book from Jake Lorenzo. Chuy's Burrito Palace catered lunches. There was always good music playing, and lots of teasing and joking, usually in Spanish. And every day, on every job, Jake Lorenzo was there. Need to dig the sewer line, Jake had a shovel. Need to cut the trim for the windows, Jake had the saw. Need to level the door, Jake brought the shims. Jake was there when workers arrived. He was there when they left, and all day he worked side by side.

At the start of the job, workers would fling cut bits of lumber on the ground. They'd toss their empty coke cans, and leave the strips of tarpaper where they fell. Jake Lorenzo quietly picked up the pieces of wood, put them in the back of his truck, and delivered them to friends to use as kindling. He picked up the cans and bottles and placed them in the recycling bins. He collected the scraps and jammed them into the trashcan.

And he picked up nails. Jake Lorenzo pulled nails from braces. He used the cat's paw to dig out nails from boards. He picked up all the bent nails tossed away by the carpenters. He picked up all the nails that fell from their pouches. Jake Lorenzo ran the cleanest construction site in Sonoma Valley, and pretty soon every worker was collecting wood scraps for the kindling pile. They placed their empty cans and bottles in the recycling bins. They started talking about how there had been no flat tires on the job.

Jake Lorenzo learned something important. In this American boom-time economy featuring grapes that cost $3,000 a ton, bottles of wine that routinely sell for $50, and houses that start at $350,000, more than the wine industry is dependent on Mexicano labor. Mexicanos are pouring our cement, hammering our nails, and laying our shingles. They paint our houses, manicure our gardens, and cut down our trees. They deliver our trusses, drive our trucks, and wire our electricity.

For years we've been hearing about the Mexicano population explosion in the United States. It is upon us. In Sonoma Valley, burritos outsell sandwiches, mariachi music outblasts rap, and you better dress up when you go out on Saturday night. Highway 12 between La Morenita and McDonald's is a Mexicano neighborhood with its own stores, restaurants, butcher shops, and video stores. Its borders are defined by the burrito wagons that set up each night at opposite ends of the neighborhood, and the Sonoma Mission Inn sticks out like a tacky tourist hotel in Puerto Vallarta.

This is Jake's new neighborhood. Jake and Jakelyn's mom moved into their new house on New Year's Eve. Of course, they had a party. Another party was held on New Year's Day. A third party was held January 2. Jake explained, "Everyone has parties for New Year's. We've got to train this house the right way."

Workers who helped on the project stop by occasionally for a visit. Jake welcomes them in, and gives them a drink. "It's their house, too," says Jake.

From time to time people stop by to ask Jake if he will manage their building projects for them. "Thanks for the offer," Jake replies, "but you can't afford me."

"We'll pay whatever you want," they say.

"See," says Jake Lorenzo. "You really can't afford me."

HARD
TIMES

Jake Lorenzo is a private eye. Private eyes hate surprises. We're supposed to know stuff. We're not supposed to get surprised. But when you build your own house, there are a couple of big surprises. The first surprise is when you finish the house, you move in, and you realize there are no window coverings. This is no big deal when you are a wealthy winery owner living behind hand wrought mechanical gates on your multi-acre homestead, but in Jake Lorenzo's neighborhood, where houses are shoehorned together tighter than blow-out chardonnays in the local grocery, it gets dicey.

Jakelyn's mother was fuming, that's for sure. Shades, drapes, and curtains are all things Jake Lorenzo took for granted until I had to buy some. Damn things are expensive, and you don't even know you need them until all the money is gone paying for incidentals like lumber, plumbing, windows, and drywall. Anyway, you shop around, take a few extra jobs, and bit by bit the windows get covered. You expand your privacy. You get a respite in the abuse from your female partner, who evidently thinks of window coverings even before there is a house design.

The windows get covered. You light a roaring fire in the new fireplace. You sit down with a nice glass of wine, and open the day's mail. That's when you get hit with the second surprise—property tax. Until now, Jake Lorenzo has been a life long renter. I had no idea about property tax, let alone supplemental tax, interim tax, whimsical tax, and just-one-more-tax.

Jake Lorenzo can feel the rest of you smirking. You're thinking, "What a schmuck. The great wine detective doesn't even cover his windows, and he's never paid property tax. Welcome to the real world Mr. Detective."

Don't misunderstand me. Jake Lorenzo is not asking for your sympathy. One way or another I'll come up with King Bush's tithe. It's just that all these financial challenges revealed a great truth of human nature. No one gives a damn about your petty troubles. They are too busy worrying about their own.

Back in the late seventies and early eighties when the California wine business really took off, it was people who had a love affair with wine who made it happen. Salesmen bored with selling the differences between Seagram's 7 Crown and Canadian Club, reveled in selling the differences between Napa, Sonoma, and Mendocino. Retailers who for years had been searching among low-end foreign wines for something with a hint of fruit, fell in love with those California fruit monsters, most of which were under

$10. Consumers, most of whom knew nothing of wine, jumped on the band-wagon, took classes, went to tastings, and bought case after case of their favorite brands.

The California wine boom took off, and the great thing about it was that everyone worked together to make it happen. Winemakers spent time talking to retailers and their clerks, to restaurateurs and their waiters. We were all in this thing together. Friendships were forged. Loyalty was in abundance.

When the boom of the nineties came, the whole thing stratified. It wasn't enough to sell all of your wine for a neat little profit. Wine had to be sold in the right restaurants to the important people for top dollar. Tightening allo-cations meant that many loyal retailers who had supported wineries for years were cut off, since marketing directors decided it was more important to be on a list at Restaurant ChiChi instead of on the shelf at Joe's Neighborhood Wine Shop. Greed set in, prices skyrocketed and those consumers who had made wine a part of their daily lives, just like we had taught them, could no longer afford our wine. They started looking for values from the Rhone, Italy, and South America, and they found great wines for reasonable prices.

So, as you sit there planning your strategy for the new year; when you consider how to expand your sales in a shrinking market; when you decide to call upon all of your loyal friends to help you through the hard times; don't expect to get a call back. No one gives a damn about your petty troubles. They are too busy worrying about their own.

There is only one way to succeed in business, even in America, the land of opportunity. If you want to be successful, you've got to do the work. The glut of grapes will be with us for years. Take advantage of it. Buy good grapes at low prices and produce delicious wines that sell at attractive prices. Get out there and press the flesh. Reconnect with retailers and their clerks and with restaurateurs and their waiters. Get out of Restaurant ChiChi and start spending time in the neighborhood joints.

Realize that people are trying to survive out there. Take the monies you've allocated for entertainment, in-house parties, and sales trips and spend it where it will do some good. Start showing up regularly at smaller restaurants that serve great food at reasonable prices. Have everyone who works at your winery go out to dinner, spend some money and leave their cards. Once res-taurateurs realize you've been supporting them, present them with delicious wines that they can sell at prices their customers can afford.

Don't give cash incentives to sales people. Give them restaurant vouch-ers to eat at local restaurants on your dime. Make sure the salesmen and the restaurants know who's picking up the tab. They will appreciate it. Stop giv-ing one on five to your retailers. Give them restaurant vouchers. Hell, retail-ers have got to eat, too. They will show their appreciation by purchasing your wines. You will jump-start your own wine economy.

The California wine business has just finished the longest extended up-cycle of its entire history. Don't pretend the money is gone. In hard times, the people who continue to spend money are heroes. Get out there and spend some money, and spend it where it will do the most good, at the neighborhood restaurants owned by hardworking people offering good value for the money. Associate your wines with the local treasured restaurants, and the locals will come to treasure your wines.

It seems obvious to Jake Lorenzo. If you live in a desert, then water is hard to come by, but we live in America, the richest country in the history of the planet. All we need to do is prime the pump.

HUNTING

Dr. Iggy Calamari and I were sitting on my porch sipping a pretty delightful Rhone. I had a .38 snub nose. Iggy held a 9mm automatic in his lap. "The bastards are going to kill everything," I said. "They've got no conscience, no moral imperative. They're prehistoric in their outlook, and they'll never change. Killing is too good for them."

"I don't know," mused Iggy. "There's something to be said for knowing your enemy, getting inside his skin so to speak."

I thought I saw some movement. I slowly raised my gun, braced my arm, carefully sighted down the barrel, and squeezed off a round. "I'll be damned if I'm getting inside the skin of some damn gopher," I shouted, "and the moles are even worse."

"Perhaps if Jakelyn's mother hadn't done such a wonderful job with the garden," suggested Iggy. "I mean it's a veritable Garden of Eden in here. Looks like you've been here for years. Can't you live and let live."

Jake Lorenzo shook his head. "What's wrong with you, Calamari? These rodents kill a few more of Jakelyn's mother's plants and neither one of us will be left alive." I fired two quick rounds at some movement over by the newly sprouted tulips. "You better start using that gun, or she'll throw your butt out of the Garden of Eden and onto Highway 12 at rush hour."

Jake Lorenzo always gets a little testy in between false spring and true spring. I think it's the fact that the only sports going on right now are professional basketball and ice hockey. At least ice hockey made sense when it was in Canada and the northern tier of States. I mean they had all of that snow anyway, might as well do something with it. But ice hockey in California, Arizona, Texas? Come on, and the only thing more futile than regular season professional basketball is a winery sales consultant during boom times.

Yes sir, March Madness can't come soon enough for Jake Lorenzo. The Final Four is one of my favorite sporting events. You know why? Because as soon as it is over, baseball season starts.

If you have any true wine business in your soul, then you are a baseball fan. The entire season coincides with harvest. Spring training starts just as the vines start sprouting. The real season starts at bud break. By July there are front-runners, and everyone thinks they know what will happen, but usually they're wrong. It's the same as people giving vintage predictions in the summer. The pennant races and the post season come during harvest.

I remember the World Series by vintage. 1977 was my first in Sonoma. I sat hand-stemming Old Hill Ranch zinfandel while listening to the Yankee-

Dodger series. No wine person will ever forget 1989. It was the year from hell; rained forever. The year Tracy Toovey was murdered. The "earthquake series." But it was also the year you had to pick a side. You were either for the Giants or the A's, one or the other, National League or American League. Jake Lorenzo is National League all the way. You can take the designated hitter and stick it with white zinfandel for all I care.

1996 created a fat, ripe, high-alcohol vintage and a great, emotional series. Joe Torre's first as Yankee manager. Just a year earlier he'd been in my garage helping me label Guerrilla Vino. Then, with his brother in the hospital, losing the first two games at home, Joe brings them back to kill off the Braves. This last year was historical. Harvest took off like a prairie fire. Grapes were coming early and in torrents. Then came September 11th, and everything seemed to stop. Sugars stuck, the weather turned cold. Grapes just hung as if in mourning. When the harvest dragged to its conclusion, we were able to focus on one of the most improbable and exciting post-seasons ever. Joe's resilient Yankees came back time after time, until Randy Johnson and Curt Schilling finally stopped them.

Wine and baseball go hand in hand. More than most things about American life, they both reflect a daily, ongoing, pastoral sense. Each year means you have to start over. Each vintage you have to do it again. In both endeavors, a lot of individual effort needs to blend into teamwork to achieve success. And both wine and baseball need to restrain their greed to let the true spirit shine through.

The wine business has always been cyclical, and we have just finished the longest, biggest, most exhilarating upswing of Jake Lorenzo's lifetime. Grape and wine prices escalated exponentially, and everyone tried to jump onto the bandwagon. Anyone with two or three acres planted grapes. Anyone with grapes started a winery. Every bottle, it seemed, had a $50 price tag.

Well, the dam has broken, the balloon has popped, and the bubble has burst. All of those rookie farmers with their two and three acre vineyards are going to have a hell of a time convincing some winery to buy their grapes. Grape prices are going down, because there's no sense in buying what you can't sell. Most wineries won't be sitting at home taking orders for their allocations this year. Someone is going to have to get out there and sell the stuff.

Marketing and programming will make a comeback. There will be more dollars and kickbacks and payoffs floating around the wine business than sunflower seeds in the Yankee dugout. One on ten: in your dreams. One on five: just gets you in the door. Hard times are a comin', like a Randy Johnson fastball in the bottom of the ninth inning.

You know in any disaster, there are the people who get reamed and there are the people who get spared. Whatever happens in an economy bankrupts some, but enriches others. In the wine business the tables are turning. The consumer is about to have his day in the sun.

Jake Lorenzo has a great idea. How about making fine wine at a fair price. That's right, get over yourself. Take those Rhone Rangers and run 'em out of town. Then blend up all those Rhone varietals and give me something for $10. Tell those Italian Super-Tuscan imitators to take all that thin, acidic sangiovese and blend it with some cabernet until they can give me an $8 wonder. I mean Chianti was supposed to be wine for the people. Take the price of your zin back down to $15 and try to keep the alcohol below 16%. If I want port, I'll let you know.

And just to show you, I'm willing to help out, I'll give you this sales lead for free. Take all that chardonnay and merlot you can't sell and give it to major league baseball. Let them sell it at the parks for $3 a glass instead of that stuff that comes in boxes. Use it as a public relations ploy. Let people see that wine should be an everyday sort of thing. Teach baseball fans that wine actually tastes good, and you'll be building yourself a future market. They could be the very consumers who turn the wine tide back to the upswing.

But then, again, what do I know? I'm just a private eye sitting on my porch with my old friend Dr. Iggy Calamari. I'm feeling a lot better though, because Iggy just showed me something. He took one of his wine-powered pacemakers and stuck it down a gopher hole. He turned on the sprinklers and watered the yard for ten minutes. Then he charged up that pacemaker with a bottle of Sonoma Mountain cabernet. I thought I could hear the gophers screaming.

Spring is almost here. The gophers are on the run. Wine prices should be coming down, although it won't happen fast enough for Jake Lorenzo. On top of that, it's baseball season. Life is good. Batter up.

LABOR DAY

From time to time, Jake Lorenzo enjoys sitting on his porch ruminating about things. Wine country is an amazing part of the world. Just look at Jakelyn's mother's garden. Actually, it's more of a botanical park than a garden. Neighbors stop their cars when they see Jake Lorenzo out in the yard. They roll down their windows and shout, "We love what you've done to the property. It's just beautiful."

When I invite them into the yard to check it out, they hesitate, but then timidly leave their cars and wander into the garden. Jakelyn's mother has a theory she applies to her garden. "I don't want to see dirt." So visitors are a bit overwhelmed by the sheer density of vegetation. A cacophony of color bursts from every corner. The bright deep red dahlias define the summer garden, but giant yellow, purple and variegated dahlias make their presence known. Giant clusters of golden daisies, mountains of blue salvia, rainbows of gladiolas, and the enormous green goddess lilies vie for notice.

Two giant palm trees tower above the garden on the street. There are dwarf peach trees, lemon trees, limes, kumquats and olives. The closer you look, the more you see. There are delicate lavender garlic flowers that find their way into our salads. There are reds and whites and purples and yellows, all flowers whose names Jake Lorenzo can't remember. There are so many different shades of green that no artist's palette could do justice to half of it.

For the entire summer, every friend who visits goes home with a bouquet. Jake Lorenzo is not talking about a bunch of flowers here. When Jakelyn's mother puts together a bouquet, it is a stunning, mind boggling, hernia inducing stack of cut flowers bursting with color and aroma. Jake Lorenzo is sure that all of our enormous health insurance bills could be paid if Jakelyn's mother would simply sell her bouquets on the corner at Highway 12.

Labor Day weekend marks the official end to summer, but not in Jakelyn's mother's garden, and not in the wine country. Unless you toil making sparkling wine, Labor Day pretty much marks the beginning of harvest. Here in Sonoma, Labor Day weekend is also the time for the annual Sonoma Valley Wine Auction.

The Sonoma Valley Wine Auction is a wild and crazy affair, serving as a reminder of the truly wonderful past, when Sonoma's winemakers joyfully hijacked trains, kidnapped celebrities, played baseball, and drank a little more each day than the city of Paris on a national holiday. Now, all these years later, the antics at the event seem a little less genuine, a bit forced, and just a tad silly. That said, Jake Lorenzo would rather attend the Sonoma Valley Wine Auction with its irreverent, fun-loving attitude, than any of those other hoity-toity affairs with their black tie this and their long pants that.

Still, auctions just aren't Jake Lorenzo's cup of tea. I'm all for charity, and I'm sure that the money raised at these events goes to great causes, like the local hospital, and housing for vineyard workers and such, but I get uncomfortable with the amounts of money people spend at wine auctions. A case of $200 wine will go for two thousand dollars. Lunch with a winemaker will go for six thousand. Believe me, Jake Lorenzo has had lunch with plenty of winemakers. In most cases they should be paying the guests to dine with them.

Wine auctions occur over several days. The auction itself is the big deal, but each day has special dinners, tours, lectures, and tastings. The cost for each individual event is far beyond the ability of any cellar rat to attend, let alone a vineyard worker. So an auction held on a weekend that honors laborers, but priced in such a way as to exclude the very workers who make the whole thing possible, is difficult for Jake Lorenzo to digest.

There is probably more stuff going on in Northern California on Labor Day weekend than any other time of the year. In addition to wine auctions, revelers can attend concerts, plays, festivals, car rallies, races, lectures, parades, baseball games or even football. The choices are endless, and the headlining talent available is staggering in its widespread appeal. As much as I love the rural charm of Sonoma, I decided to take Jakelyn's mom and a group of friends to an urban experience this Labor Day Weekend. So, this year we opted for Oakland's Art & Soul festival.

The Art & Soul festival takes place in downtown Oakland. You can take BART, get off at the downtown exit, and walk straight into the Blues Stage in the heart of City Center. Art & Soul features five stages and more than fifty different acts each day. There are local dance groups, world music, blues, jazz, gospel, reggae and R&B. This year's headliners included Ziggy Marley, Guster, Matt Nathanson, Rachelle Ferrell, Pete Escovedo, Jules Broussard, and John Lee Hooker Jr. And the whole event is FREE.

In the same way that New Orleans began the French Quarter festival to entice locals back to the French Quarter, the City of Oakland sponsors the Art & Soul festival to show visitors the new downtown Oakland, and to celebrate what they call "the most culturally diverse city in America." The Art & Soul crowd is certainly diverse: black, white, Chicano, Asian, wealthy, poor, middle class, young and old. People came casual, dressed up, and in costume. At Oakland's Art & Soul festival there is as much diversity in the people attending as there is among the flowers in Jakelyn's mother's garden. And the whole event is FREE.

For ten blocks in and around City Hall the streets are teeming with people shopping at shops featuring colorful hemp dragons, Shona sculpture, ethnic clothing and fine art. There are murals for children, a kid zone, and art for kids. There's a literature tent, with speakers, poetry readings and the American Book Awards. In a great civilized show of confidence, booths sold beer and wine, (two buck Chuck for $4 a glass, here's a wine country opportunity just waiting to happen), and people were allowed to wander through the fair sipping their beverages.

I'm not trying to get sappy here, but in a time when people don't seem able to get along, where people show no understanding of their neighbor's religious or personal beliefs, where people strap explosives to their bodies and blow themselves up to make a point, what is it worth to have people of all walks of life hanging out and enjoying themselves at an event sponsored by their own local government?

For Jake Lorenzo and his friends, this year's Labor Day was spent with working people. People of all races, creeds, and classes came together at an event sponsored by their tax dollars. The event signaled the end of summer or the beginning of harvest, depending upon your point of view. Either way, the City of Oakland did a great thing for a great many people, and Jake Lorenzo was glad to have been invited.

GRAPEVINES AND GRANDBABIES

Jake Lorenzo sits in a Seattle hospital. I'm fine, but Jakelyn is screaming in the next room. Her mother is with her. So is her husband. It's nothing to worry about; Jakelyn is having another baby.

The due date was the 12th, and Jakelyn's mother insisted we arrive on that very day. "Jakelyn will need us at the hospital, and to watch the grandbaby," she says. "It's always good to have family around during labor."

Personally, this makes no sense to Jake Lorenzo, who knows in his soul of souls that the last place a man should hang out is in the proximity of a woman in labor. Women in labor have no patience for men, and Jake Lorenzo also knows that it's a myth when women tell each other, "The second one is much easier."

Jake may not know much, but I do know that if you try to pull something that weighs more than six pounds out of your body, it is going to hurt like hell, and previous experience is not going to make it easier.

It's been nine years since Jakelyn had our first grandbaby. When Jakelyn and her husband had a talk with her to tell her that she would soon have a baby sister, the grandbaby sat quietly taking it all in. She thoughtfully walked up the stairs toward her room, as her parents watched. When she got to the landing she turned and said, "I've enjoyed being an only child."

So while Jakelyn's mother and husband shepherd her through the birth of my new grandchild, I have the great good fortune of hanging out with Jakelyn's ex-only child. She is a very independent kid who spends untold hours watching the Animal Channel and is full of information on the eating habits of wolves, the mating rituals of elephants, and all things about dolphins. She's also a sharp dresser with a unique style sense. It's sort of retro-Cyndi Lauper with toe socks.

We're taking turns reading to each other. She's reading some horrific story about a house cat that gets left behind during a beach vacation, and is forced to survive out in the wilds. I'm reading horrific excerpts from Fast Food Nation trying to ensure that she stays away from processed food in our nation's drive-throughs.

At one point, my eldest granddaughter stops reading, looks at her grandfather and says, "I guess things are going to change, right Paw Paw."

Jake Lorenzo gives her a hug. "Things always change, that's what keeps life interesting."

Speaking of change, have you given any thought to wine grapes lately? Jake Lorenzo has lived in Sonoma for 25 years, and I've seen a whole lot of change. I'm not talking about over-planting vineyards or the disappearance of apple, pear and prune trees. I'm not talking about which varieties are planted, what the prices are, or who's not selling grapes. Jake Lorenzo is talking about the actual grapes themselves. Things in the vineyard have changed radically, and that has affected the way wines are made dramatically.

Back in the late 1970's and into the 1980's most vineyards were dry-farmed. The rootstock was St. George, although by 1980 growers were shifting to AXR-1. Irrigation, when used, was either flood irrigation or overhead sprinklers about once or twice during the growing season. Grapevines had thick gnarled trunks, and were either head-pruned or cane-pruned. Grapevines believed themselves to be living in some scene from *Dune*, parched in the desert hoarding every last drop of water, wasting no moisture.

The great Phylloxera debacle of the late 1980's led to massive replanting. That replanting coincided with new clones, new rootstocks, and widespread drip irrigation. Today, grapevines rise up on spindly trunks and spread out into a wide assortment of trellis configurations. They are jam packed, fighting one another for space. Today's grapevines act like tourists at a trendy beach who only need to motion the cabana boys for another drink.

Thirty years ago, grapes ripened with good flavors around 23 or 24° Brix. Once picked, they came into the winery, acids were bumped with tartaric and fermenting temperatures for reds ran between 80–85° F. Fermentations rarely stuck, and malolactic went through easily and completely.

Nowadays, grapes "don't taste right" until 27 or 28° Brix. They get picked, come to the winery, get a hit of DAP and yeast food, and ferment at 90–95°F. They struggle with high alcohol, have a miserable time finishing fermentation and malolactic is often an ongoing nightmare that lasts well into the following spring.

Jake Lorenzo is not a viticulturist, but I am a hell of a private eye. In my line of work good detectives know to keep things simple and to follow the money. Rookie private eyes waste a lot of time running the labyrinths of deception. The grizzled veteran steps back and tries to follow the simple basics.

When it comes to grapes, the simple basics are to get the things ripe before the rains come, and to keep the winemakers happy. If you can deliver grapes that have deep color and rich flavors, then you are perceived to be a good grower. Maybe a little common sense would be helpful.

Common sense tells Jake Lorenzo that high density in the vineyard might be a good idea in rich, valley soils where runaway vigor is a problem. Plant the vines close to one another, and have them compete for nutrients and water. I see where this could be beneficial. I do not understand why you would use this same scheme on hills, or shallow clay soils where the extra competition may deplete the few nutrients and moisture available to the plants in the first place.

I can see where a farmer would love the convenience of drip irrigation. To a farmer, good irrigation is an insurance policy that contributes to many a good night's sleep. It makes sense that more efficient, regular watering of plants could develop healthier plants and better tasting fruit. But I have to wonder about 8–10 gallons per week from June through harvest.

In the last couple of years, I've seen these new rootstocks shut down, almost out of spite. It's as if they are saying, "No more drinks, please. I've got a hangover." Watching their vineyards shut down causes farmers to panic, so they are experimenting with foliar sprays to hasten ripening. "A little potassium never hurt anything," they say. Jake Lorenzo says follow the money. A lot of it is being spent on chemicals and consultants.

Once again, I'm not a viticulturist, but maybe it would be better to use a little less water and spread it out over the growing season. Try to use plant density to take advantage of your particular growing conditions. Regulate crop size to help ripen the grapes. Be as natural as possible. Don't be spraying things onto your plants and into your soil until you know what it is going to do, and what the long-term effects will be. In short, try to simplify everything in the vineyard.

Jake Lorenzo is not a winemaker either, but does it make sense to strive for intensity and extraction by letting fruit get very ripe, and then diluting it with water once it gets to the winery? Does all the chemical manipulation necessary to finish high-alcohol fermentations make better wine, or are you just treating the symptoms?

It could make more sense to work with your grower to get ripe flavors at lower sugars. That would reduce the alcohol, and problems with stuck fermentation and retarded malolactic. If nothing else, think of the money you could save in taxes if your wines were under 14% alcohol.

Jake Lorenzo is not a viticulturist or a winemaker, but I am a Grandpa for the second time. I'm going to sit with my family, open a good bottle of sparkling wine, and read my grandbaby a story.

DAD

It was one of those crystal clear nights so rare to Southern California. Jake Lorenzo gazed out the window of the Southwest 737 at the coastline wrapped around the Los Angeles basin where millions of golden lights flickered and sparkled in the night. A voluptuous full moon rose majestically in the East, as the last magenta streaks faded from a spectacular sunset in the West. It occurred to Jake Lorenzo, on this remarkable night, as the plane made its approach toward John Wayne Airport, that transportation had progressed quite a bit since 1922.

*   *   *

It was on a moonless night in 1922 that my father and his family made their escape from Russia. My father was a bit shy of his first birthday when he boarded a rickety boat with his mother and father and aunt and tried paddling through the night, across a dark, muddy river to freedom. My father's two brothers had starved to death the previous year, and my grandfather had already been arrested twice for making escape attempts. The third time was the charm. It had better be, 'cause when the Czar's police caught you the third time, they executed you.

There, in the pitch of night, on a mucky boat crossing a muddy river, my father began to cry. Terrified of the chilling consequences of being discovered during a third escape attempt, my grandparents were about to drown my father, because they could not stop his crying, and they knew his crying would lead the border guards to them, and they would be shot. Fortunately, my aunt took my father and began to play with him. He stopped crying, and was saved.

*   *   *

My father survived that trip, went on to America, married and had a mostly wonderful, but always adventurous life. My father was also the longest living survivor of ocular melanoma in the United States. Then they tried to kill him.

Melanoma, or skin cancer, seems innocuous enough. I mean, no one actually dies of cancer on their skin. The problem with melanoma is that lesions on the skin are simply markers of cancerous cells traveling throughout the body. Sooner or later the melanoma metastasizes in a body organ, usually the brain or the liver, and death is pretty quick, but never sweet.

Eight years after laser surgery for ocular melanoma, doctors found melanoma in my Dad's liver. They discovered the cancer by accident, and because they found it early, before the onset of debilitating symptoms, they went in and surgically removed a large portion of my Dad's liver.

Since Jake Lorenzo knows it's just a matter of time before I'll need one, I've made several friendships with doctors trained in the art of liver transplants. They helped out, and my Dad's operation was deemed a "surgical success."

It was during the post-operative recuperation that they tried to kill him. An intern, or resident, or other designated inexperienced, overworked health care professional incorrectly inserted a tube. They meant to relieve a build up of fluid, but accidentally put the tube into my Dad's lung. A tube in your lung makes it very difficult to breathe, sort of like shoveling a tank full of red pomace and trying to survive in that CO_2 environment. My mother dragged a doctor into the room. He removed the tube and placed it correctly, but the event caused my Dad to lose confidence, and he had a major sinker.

I ended up sitting beside him for the next three days with my gun on my lap. Whenever anyone came in to tube my Dad, or take blood, or check his staples, I cocked the trigger and very quietly asked them to detail the particular procedure as they went through it. It proved an effective remedy for inadvertent acts of murder. My Dad rallied, recovered and went on to see his granddaughter, Jakelyn, get married.

Dad got off a great line at the wedding. Someone was talking to him about the fact that he had three sons, and each had one daughter. The friend asked my father if it bothered him that the Lorenzo name would not continue. "Hell, Lorenzo isn't my name anyway, its Laurenzitison. Why should I care if some customs official's misspelling of my family name continues?"

Now, on this remarkable night, Jake Lorenzo and his brothers are sitting on Dad's bed saying good-bye. My Dad is very weak, and dozes off repeatedly, but in those precious moments of wakefulness, he is coherent. He recognizes me and my brothers. He is not in pain. Finally, he closes his eyes, falls asleep, and dies.

*   *   *

I know that none of this has much to do with the wine business, but it has occurred to me that one can tell a lot about people from observing their wine cellars. Wine cellars often reflect the way a person lives his life. Some people have no patience, they drink up all the bottles they were trying to save, rushing through the wines and life and never taking the time to savor either. Other people build giant cellars only to watch their favorites die horrible deaths before they get around to opening them. They live their lives the same way, spending all their time working for some day that may never come. Far better in life and in wine, to have a large eclectic cellar, to dip into it regularly and often, to sample wines and life in their youth and enjoy their growth and development into maturity.

When you think of it, drinking a bottle of wine is the end of the line for the grapes in that bottle. On rare occasions a magical bottle lives, grows and matures, and then gives itself up at that precise right moment, and it becomes etched indelibly in our hearts and our memories.

If Jake Lorenzo's Dad was a bottle of wine, he would have been that magic bottle.

PART III

ON THE ROAD

Wine Tasting in Europe

Spanish Anniversary

A Spanish Meal

In Hot Water

Oregon Vacation

Dreams and Consequences

The Tequila Life

The Stuff with the Worm

Minister of Culture

Garbage

Simple Pleasures

Jake Lorenzo's Guide to New Orleans

WINE TASTING IN EUROPE

"God dammit, Iggy. Are you trying to kill me?"

"Jake," says Dr. Iggy Calamari, "are you wussing out on me?"

"You've got a lot of nerve, Iggy. Being a wuss is one thing, but we've been eating and drinking enough to feed a small village."

"I know, I know," says Dr. Calamari, "It's the French paradox in action. You make a great medical subject, and you're helping me make money.

"This is the best research gig I've ever had," he continues. "Basically, I invite friends to great restaurants where we eat and drink as much as we can. I do a few simple blood tests, make astute observations that inevitably imply that wine is good for your health, and then the Wine Institute spends millions publicizing my research, not to mention putting me up here in Paris."

"It's old news," replies Jake Lorenzo, private eye. "I don't even open that crap from the Wine Institute anymore. Their press releases sound more like rehashes from medical journals than wine news."

"It's not my fault," whines Iggy, "I'm not about to kill the goose that laid the golden foie gras. Besides, the Wine Institute is picking up the damn tab."

"Fine Iggy," I say. "Do what you have to do, but there's no way in hell we're ordering fromage."

Iggy grins, "Suit yourself, Jake. We'll skip the cheese, but you'll have to try a bit of the crème brulée. I've got a whole new research program dedicated to egg yolks. Those egg people have gotten a bad rap from the medical community about cholesterol. They've hired me to turn that perception around.

"Besides, this wine thing won't last forever."

*   *   *

After feeding me to the point of bursting, and then the next day taking enough blood to deflate me like a balloon, Dr. Calamari stuffed me into his silver Citroen and we took off for Belgium.

"Now, listen to me Jake. Belgium is the land of beer. We'll be drinking stuff that makes Guinness taste like water. The stuff is like 12% alcohol, so three or four of them give you a pretty good buzz. Strictly as a prophylactic measure I'm going to take you to lunch, so you don't have to drink on an empty stomach."

"I can't do it, Iggy. I can't eat again. You almost killed me last night."

"That's the beauty of Belgium, Jake. We won't be messing around with rich foods, or heavy sauces. We'll just have a bowl of mussels. Fresh, in a nice broth, they'll be perfect. Of course, they always come with a plate of fries, but then fries were invented in Belgium, and you 'got to go with the flow,' right."

Jake Lorenzo is no idiot, and I know that it's useless talking to Dr. Calamari when he's like this. If he wants to eat mussels and fries, while we pound a few beers, I'll humor him. After all, he's the one who wrangled me an invitation to one of the best wine tastings in all of Belgium: Wijnagentuur Vincent.

This tasting, held every other year, is hosted by Marc and Anneke Buelincx. They and their company, Wijnagentuur Vincent, have put together a remarkable portfolio of wineries from little known regions of France and Italy. Marc is thin and wiry and seems to hover in space with a barely controlled energy. His wife, Anneke, appears to be the calming influence until you get to know her and recognize that she shares Marc's high-speed obsession.

And that obsession is wine; good wine for a very reasonable price. Wine with character, delineated flavor, firm structure, and fair prices. Wines that perfectly represent their regions of origin. Wines that seamlessly enhance the local cuisine. Wines that make an evening, or long afternoon, while barely denting your pocket book. Delicious wines, that are—have I mentioned this—incredibly cheap. Kermit Lynch, eat your heart out. Bobby Katcher, ain't even close. When it comes to great wines at incredible prices from places no one's ever heard of, Marc Buelincx is the man.

A wine tasting in Belgium is refreshing. No one talks about how good wine is for your health. People are too busy smoking cigarettes and eating paté. Rows of tables spread through the giant room. Each table represents a different winery, and the owner of that winery proudly stands behind that table pouring his wares.

Some of Marc's finds have been discovered by the likes of Robert Parker and Stephen Tanzer, like Clavel and Laffitte Teston, but they still come to the Belgian tasting. It's more a sign of respect for Marc and his faith in them than a genuine attempt to sell wine.

The wines are fantastic. There's a tremendous cherried Roussillon from Forca Real; a powerfully delightful Montpeyroux from Domaine Saint Andrieu made entirely from mouvedre grapes. Another Roussillon from Domaine Mas Cremat exudes fruit and good acidic structure, until the Pic Saint Loup from Chateau L'Euziere fills my tastebuds with unctuous fruit. The Madirans attack with their barbed tannins, but the rich cloak of ripe fruit and earthy texture proves too seductive to scare me off. There is a Bandol from Domaine La Tour du Bon that is a revelation, and a Cotes de Duras from Chateau Moliere that could single-handedly make the region famous.

Jake Lorenzo has himself one hell of a good time. Oh, and by the way, each of these wines retails in Belgium for under $10 US.

That night, Marc and Anneke take the whole bunch of us out to dinner. Vignerons from all over France and Italy pass each other their wines and tell stories about harvesting grapes, and fixing broken equipment, and having a fine meal. These are not people who dine in fancy restaurants. They eat great food at home, and in their villages. These are not people who spend fortunes on bottles of famous wines. They drink wonderful wines made with their own hands from their own grapes, grown on their own land.

Selling wine is more than just business for these people. It is essential if they are to continue their very way of life. Marc and Anneke Buelincx found them, encouraged them, and sold their wine when nobody wanted to buy it. They helped contribute to the survival of the vigneron's way of life.

Jake Lorenzo hopes there's a Marc Buelincx somewhere in America. I hope he's out there talking to growers we don't yet know, encouraging them to make wonderful wines at fair prices. I hope he's teaching them that a way of life may be of more value than succeeding as a great American business.

If you are out there, I wish you'd get in touch with Jake Lorenzo, because I'd love to support someone making honest wine for an honest price for the everyday table. Until then, God bless you, and drink Belgian beer. The stuff is incredible.

But right now, I've got to defend myself. Dr. Iggy Calamari has just entered the restaurant with a four-foot cart filled with a gigantic crème brulée. He can do whatever he wants to all these winemakers. He's not taking my blood again.

SPANISH ANNIVERSARY

Iknow it dates me, but Jake Lorenzo and Jakelyn's mom are celebrating 30 years together. That makes us the most enduring couple in the private eye business. Left to her own devices, Jakelyn's mom would celebrate this historic event by sleeping in. The lady knows how to sleep.

All of our friends know better than to call the house before nine o'clock in the morning. She calls it the nine o'clock rule. Usually she'll stumble into the kitchen to start coffee around ten. Then she'll lie around watching horrible reruns on TV, drinking coffee until almost noon. From there, she's off to lunch. All in all, not a bad life, but to commemorate 30 years, Jake Lorenzo feels obligated to do something special.

So, we went to Spain... for a month.

Spain is a wonderful country, filled with gorgeous villages clinging to cliffs overlooking the ocean, contrasted with stark barren plateaus dotted with Moorish estates on the inland plateaus. Beer is served cold. Wine is plentiful and inexpensive. Food is unique, delicious, and served all day long. And the people, well, pound for pound they are the eatingest, drinkingest people on the planet.

We spent the bulk of our time in Basque country and the Rioja area. For the most part, these are decidedly non-tourist areas, especially in early March when we were there. Basque country is known to have the finest food in all of Spain, although we avoided the great food shrines of Akelaré and Arzak with dedicated fervor. No, Michelin star-studded fancy restaurants are not for Jake Lorenzo, even on an anniversary. (Besides, I brought neither tie nor a jacket.) We chose instead those tiny, proprietor-owned bars and restaurants that fuel the Spanish dining scene.

Eating and drinking in Spain is serious business, and it takes a little study to get things right. The bars open around ten o'clock in the morning. They call them bars, but they are really the heart and soul of Spanish dining. All bars serve *tapas*, and most bars are known for a particular specialty. The bars close at three in the afternoon, then reopen at six in the evening. They stay open until midnight during the week and until three or four in the morning on weekends. Most are open seven days a week. Restaurants, on the other hand, open at one or two in the afternoon, close at five or six, then reopen at nine in the evening. No self-respecting Spaniard would ever sit down to dinner before ten o'clock.

When Jakelyn's mom and I would start bar-hopping, we'd have a *corto* of beer. A *corto* or *cortito* is the smallest size beer at about 4 ounces. From there you have a *caña*, a *tubo*, and a *jarra*, which takes you all the way up to a sixteen-ounce mug. Prices for a *corto* start at 75 pesetas (35¢ US) and go up to 300 pesetas ($1.75 US) for a *jarra*. We'd wander from one bar to the next, sipping *cortos* of cold beer until one of the *tapas* struck our fancy. Perhaps a nice *tortilla* (omelet), made with pimento peppers and tuna, or some deviled egg topped with green and red peppers.

Once we got some food in our stomach, we switched to wine. Wine (*vino*) is *blanco* (white), *rosado* (rose), or *tinto* (red). Of course, *tinto* was the only Spanish word Jakelyn's mom bothered to learn. Bars serve wines of the region exclusively, and the wine is priced according to age. While you can order a six-ounce glass of wine, the locals prefer the two-ounce pour called a *copita*. *Vino cosecha* or *vino joven* is wine from the current vintage and sells for 50–80 pesetas (25–40¢ US). *Vino crianza*, a step up in aging costs 80–150 pesetas (40–90¢). *Reservas*, which are vintage dated, start at 150 pesetas (90¢).

We'd wander from bar to bar, drinking our *copitas de vino* and sampling various *tapas*. This turned out to be the missing secret of *tapas*. The American concept is to go to a single *tapas* restaurant, and order a series of small dishes until all the flavors run together and you can't remember one dish from another. In Spain, they go to a series of restaurants and order a single dish at each one. Each night of *tapas* dining is a community event. Most of the bars are congregated in a small district so the locals wander from place to place encountering their friends, relatives, and neighbors. This bar is famous for fried calamari; the next for stuffed peppers; the third has the best *chorizo*, and so on.

Tapas dining exists every day in every part of Spain. From San Sebastian to Madrid, from Segovia to Barcelona, from every small town to every big city, *tapas* bars are filled with people eating and drinking. You can walk into an empty bar, and be guaranteed that it will be full within ten minutes any night of the week. Fifteen minutes later, it may be empty again according to the ebb and flow of people wandering through the district.

Weekends bring El Niño like tidal waves of people to the bars and restaurants. Friday and Saturday nights find every bar seething with loads of teens and college kids sipping wine, sampling plates of food and swaying to pulsating disco music. On Sundays the bars fill up with families. Grandparents drink with their kids, and smile as their grandchildren run through the bar. Baby carriages provide moving obstacle courses, and still people eat and drink, moving from one bar to another.

Spanish bars are wonderful. They are synonymous with good food, fine drink, and camaraderie. More than that, they provide a sense of community for each town, village and city. In 27 days of drinking and eating, in hundreds of bars throughout Spain, Jake Lorenzo never encountered a drunk, never saw a fight, never even heard a loud argument.

It's all so damn civilized.

America could learn a lesson from Spain. I think the nineteen bars and restaurants around the square in Sonoma should have *tapas* from 4–8 p.m. every evening. Sell *copitas* of wine for 50¢ to $1. Sell small plates of local delicacies. Have soft drinks and juice free for the kids. Get all those retirees to drink and eat alongside the yuppies and the Gen-X crowd, and let them all watch the kids romp around for a few hours.

Remind us that family, food, and wine are a holy trinity of life.

That would be something Jake Lorenzo and Jakelyn's mom would love to see. Hell, if they can pull that off, we may stick around for another 30 years.

A SPANISH MEAL

When it comes to gourmet dining, rice is not the first dish that pops into Jake Lorenzo's addled brain. As much as I love Mexican food, I have never seen the charm in Mexican rice. It's too plain with its bit of tomato and onion. Everyone knows that for Jake Lorenzo, New Orleans is food Mecca, but you won't see me passing up barbecued shrimp, or paneed rabbit for some jambalaya hodge podge.

For the most part, I see rice as a condiment. You know, something to hold my red beans. A dollop to cool down my gumbo. Filler to hold the ingredients in my sushi. So you can imagine my surprise, when I found out that Jake Lorenzo loves paella.

In Spain, rice is not a dish; it's a national treasure. And in Valencia, where paella originated, Spaniards look upon rice with a fervor that is unnerving to even the toughest of private eyes. Jake Lorenzo believes most people in Valencia would rather have an unwelcome foreigner date their daughters, than have their rice insulted, and when it comes to rice dishes, paella is king. People argue over the nuances of preparation; how much heat to use, what size pan, when to add the water, which saffron is best, how crispy to make the bottom layer, how moist the finished product should be.

Paella is sort of like Spanish pizza. Don't get Jake Lorenzo wrong. The entire coast of Eastern Spain is loaded with plenty of mediocre pizza joints, but paella forms the function of pizza for the locals. They even have paella to go. Especially on Sundays when you see pairs of men carrying gigantic paella pans covered with tin foil up to their beach front condominiums for mid-day comida. The rice in paella is the base for the whole dish, much like pizza dough. The broth, olive oil, and saffron function as a sauce. The list of ingredients is mind boggling, and some of the combinations are hair raising.

Discussions go on for hours about which ingredients form the perfect combination for paella. Some prefer a very simple country combo of duck and chicken. Others prefer seafood heavy on shellfish with clams, mussels, shrimp and langostinos. Still others insist on weird combos like duck, eel, and snails. The amazing thing is that the ingredients never overwhelm the rice.

The rice is extraordinary. Valencian rice puts arborio rice to shame. The Chinese would probably switch to bread if they realized what they had been missing for the last 4,000 years. Valencian rice is plump, moist, and flavorful with a perfect crunchy texture. It's a sponge for flavor, and likes to get crispy on the bottom of a paella pan.

Like all great religions, paella has its shrines. One of the best is Casa Salvador in Cullera, a sleepy Mediterranean beach town about half an hour south of Valencia. Casa Salvador opened in 1950. It has never been closed a single day. Never. Not once.

It's an incredible place, beautiful in a sort of Moorish way. Pristine white walls with a dark blue tiled roof, the restaurant stretches from room to room, out onto a stunning patio overlooking the estuary. The rooms are elegantly casual, the service first rate, and the food is out of this world. Casa Salvador can seat 450 guests at one time. On a busy Sunday they serve over 2,000 meals. Jake Lorenzo has written long and often about how much he distrusts large restaurants. Casa Salvador is an exception that proves the rule. Did I mention they have more than 40,000 bottles of wine?

Paella, as a dish, creates a perfect dining experience, but you need to take friends if you are to get out alive. It takes a solid forty-five minutes to prepare paella. As long as we are going to be waiting at the table, why not enjoy ourselves? We start with a Cava, a nice, slightly nutty, sparkling wine, of which there are dozens of producers, and which can be had in restaurants at prices from $6–$20. As long as we're having some sparkling wine, why not have some oysters, or perhaps some of those incredibly fresh anchovies in a light tomato sauce. Spanish whites are making great strides. We might sip a crisp sauvignon blanc from the Penedes while we nibble on a cool, delicious grilled octopus salad, or some sardines warmed through on the grill and drizzled with olive oil.

We're forty minutes into the meal, so we should probably order our paella. We settle on the duck, mussel, snail, and cigala (a kind of shrimp) paella. Since there are only four of us, we ask for the minimum two-portion order. While we are waiting, we order one of their perfectly executed Spanish tortillas with a bottle of Les Terrasses from Priorat for just $18. Hell, the wine's only $18, we should get that platter of assorted cold cuts that looks so good.

When the gorgeous paella is brought to the table, we realize we're beginning to fill up, but what the hell, it's only rice. We order a Pesquera from Ribera del Duero for $22 while the waiter divvies up the paella. Each mouthful is absolutely delicious, bursting with flavor. There is a creamy richness to the rice, and the complex flavors of saffron, garlic, onion and olive oil are perfectly balanced. We pluck the snails from their shells using toothpicks. We use the mussel shells as pinchers to extract the meat. We tear at the cigala like we're at the Last Supper. Even the duck disappears without much fuss. We wipe our plates with bread, until they shine with a sated luster.

The waiter brings a dessert menu, but of course there is no way we can continue, until Jakelyn's mother repeats one of our favorite sayings, "If you don't eat, you die." So, we order a chocolate mousse cake and a flan to share with our coffees. And we are most pleased to accept the complimentary brandy to help our digestion.

The bill arrives, and the entire meal, with four bottles of wine, coffee and dessert, tip included, works out to about $50 per person. Don't forget that's with a very weak dollar working against the powerful Euro.

Jake Lorenzo marvels at the reasonable wine prices in Spain. At Kailuze Restaurante in Valencia, our favorite sommelier explained, "We buy the wine for $10, so we sell it for $18–$20. It is enough profit, and we will sell more than one bottle. It is better for the customer, and better for our food."

There is something remarkably civilized about a three-hour meal. The Spaniards have learned how to make that meal an affordable reality. It is Jake Lorenzo's hope that our restaurants learn this important lesson. The key for us wine drinkers is wine pricing. Serve good wines at reasonable prices. Like our friend says, "It's better for the customer, and better for the food."

IN HOT WATER

Jake Lorenzo went to China. Sure, it was about ten years ago, but China was an experience that you don't forget. It was a pretty good gig. I handled security for a pair of Sonoma Valley winemakers. They went, ostensibly to give recommendations to a wine making commune in Tsing Tao. The Chinese, desperate for foreign currency, realized that the Westerners combing their country looking for joint venture deals refused to drink Chinese wine. The leaders of this particular commune figured if they got California winemakers to teach them how to make wine from Chinese grapes that pleased Western palates, they could corner the market and collect some serious foreign currency.

Jake Lorenzo was invited along as security. Not that foreigners need security in China. "Yes, sir," the omnipresent guides would say, "China is a free country. We have nothing to hide. You may go anywhere you wish in China, but now we are going to the Great Wall."

It took the California winemakers a while to figure things out. It took Jake Lorenzo about five minutes. The winemakers thought the Chinese were seriously interested in learning California winemaking techniques. They brought gifts—some technical books, some pruning shears, and even some double-yolked turkey eggs that they mistakenly believed were highly prized by the Chinese. The Chinese, obviously to my trained eye, believed the Californians to be millionaires, and they were pretty direct in trying to get commitments of money so they could buy a new bottling line.

The wonderful aspect of devious Chinese business dealings was that they all occurred at banquets. We would spend the day touring the winery or visiting the vineyards, but each evening we were treated to an ever-expanding banquet. Course after course of Chinese delicacies was served. A selection of cold meats, followed by a soup. The ubiquitous sea slugs, abalone, clams, and mussels. Various pork and chicken dishes were always followed by a whole fish course to represent the bounty of Chinese cuisine. Once we were served a whole pig's foot. Try eating that with chopsticks.

Throughout the course of every banquet, three glasses sat in front of each participant. One was filled with beer, one with wine, and the last was filled with some distilled spirit made from sorghum. At various times through the course of the meal guests stood up to make elaborate toasts. Our government hosts, wearing their blue Mao jackets, would toast the winemakers and drink the sorghum spirit. Jake Lorenzo and the winemakers would follow suit.

This sorghum spirit smelled and tasted like a dirty clothes hamper. Immediately upon drinking the stuff, you began to belch, and the flavor repeated itself. I quickly stepped in, pulling some fine California wine out of my pack, popping the corks and pouring into the wineglasses. From then on we made our toasts using good California wine.

You see, in China verbal contracts are binding. So, our Chinese hosts were trying to get the California winemakers smashed, have them agree to fund their new bottling line, and send us on our way. Fortunately, we can out-drink the Chinese. When the host of the banquet gets too loaded, he spouts some special quote, which loosely translates to "Ollie, Ollie Oxen Free." From that time on, all business deals are off. Each night we would endure all the pointed questions about procuring bottling equipment, attempting to enlighten our hosts with winemaking specifics. "We are Chinese," they would say. "We've been making wine for 2,000 years. We don't need you to tell us how to make wine. We need a new corker."

The California winemakers would smile, shake their heads, and plunge on with more winemaking secrets, until the host would say the magic words. Then we'd eat and drink, and have a great time talking with the young student translators who accompanied us. They explained that we were shrewd business people, a talent highly prized by all Chinese, and as long as we refused to give money for the new bottling line, we would have to endure more elaborate feasts and more expensive beverages.

Money was never a question, since the winemakers didn't have any. It goes without saying, of course, that Jake Lorenzo was without funds. So we ate and drank our way through Chinese wine country, acting like shrewd businessmen, trying to impart wine knowledge. Then we said our good-byes and took off for Japan.

The one thing Jake Lorenzo has always wanted to do in Japan is experience a Japanese bath. I called a friend who was living in Tokyo, and he took us to one. We walked in with the California winemakers in tow. We turned in our clothes, sat on the little plastic stools to wash ourselves, and then we entered the bath. There were two baths: a large one filled with several Japanese men and a much smaller tub occupied by a single elderly man. The winemakers and my friend entered the larger crowded tub. Jake Lorenzo figured he might as well use the smaller tub, which was less crowded.

As I stepped into the tub, its occupant was wide-eyed. I had a fleeting thought that perhaps Jake Lorenzo had made a mistake. Perhaps the small tub was meant for one occupant at a time. But when my toe hit the water, I realized the tub was full of boiling water. The pain was exquisite, but here I was, a tough private eye from America visiting a neighborhood bath. I couldn't wimp out, so I steadily and painfully descended into the tub until the water was up to my neck. I remained there for about five minutes, hallucinating about all the crawfish I had boiled and eaten in New Orleans. Then I slowly climbed out of the tub and somehow made my way to the larger bath, where I joined my friends.

"Hot, wasn't it," said our guide. "You know I've lived in Japan for five years, but I've never been able to work my way into that tub. I don't think any of the boys will forget Jake Lorenzo too soon."

I bring this up, because Jake Lorenzo is publishing a book. I've been working with a computer wizard. I use the term "wizard" instead of "nerd", because these people have magical powers and don't exist in our temporal plane. The problem is that computer wizards have no respect for deadlines. They don't even understand the word "dead", possibly because bullets won't kill them.

Jake Lorenzo has met some pretty unsavory people. Liars, cheats, drug addicts, but I've never met anyone who could look you in the eye and lie like a computer wizard. "Sure Jake, I'll have it for you in an hour," he says four days in a row.

In my younger days, I would have lost it. I would have threatened the guy, maybe roughed him up a bit. But Jake Lorenzo has matured. I remember my time in Asia. I walk downstairs and admire the huge hot tub a friend recently gave to me. I pop open a bottle of champagne, pour a glass, and gently lower myself into the hot bubbling water. As I soak, letting the tension wash out of my body, I think, "Hot, this ain't hot. Why one time in Japan..."

OREGON VACATION

Chuy had a hot date, and they were joining us for a week in Oregon. "The play *es la cosa*," Chuy said, and his hot date cackled with laughter as if Chuy was the funniest thing since merlot rosé. Jakelyn's mom gave me a look that said it was going to be a long week.

We blasted up Highway 5 making Ashland in just under five hours. We roared directly to Omar's for cocktails and to get our clothes smelling of cigarettes. In spite of all the chi chi tourists, and the Californians buying up all the prime property, Oregon remains true to itself. Jake Lorenzo doesn't know how long it can last, but he's happy to enjoy it while he can.

The occasional tourists find their way to Omar's, but basically it remains a local place, especially the bar. Most of the locals are drinking versions of boilermakers. That is, they order a shot and a beer. But this being Oregon, the shot is usually single malt; the beer is from a local micro brew. Everyone in the place smokes cigarettes, so your eyes burn, and you develop a phobia about ever seeing the place in the light of day. When you rub the smoke out of your eyes, you can see the local tradesmen, straight from work in their dirty clothes.

Snippets of conversation float past, "Some schmuck bought the old Nelson place for $400,000."

"You've got to be shittin' me, that place ain't worth half that."

"That's the truth, and it'll take another $100 grand to fix it up."

"Tell you one thing, man, I'd sure like to have that kind of money. If I did, I'd buy me a..."

We decided we'd had enough local color. We paid our bill and stumbled outside gasping for the fresh mountain air. Revived we went downtown for a terrific dinner in a little place called Amuse. Oregon pinots were on the list for $24–$34, which seemed very reasonable to us.

After dinner, the play is the thing. Shakespeare, modern, it doesn't matter; live theater retains a special magic. Of course, Chuy complained that there were no Chicano playwrights featured. I pointed out that Octavio Solis was featured as a guest writer and was creating a play with seven actors. Chuy was so pleased that he paid for the cocktails at intermission *and* after the play.

We hung around Ashland for three days, eating modestly priced and delicious meals accompanied by affordable bottles of Oregon wines, and going to the theater. We visited a winery or two, and at one point we had to get a new windshield for my car after a logging truck flipped something up from the highway that turned it into a spider web of cracked glass.

Jakelyn's mom brought it up first, "You know, everyone here is so nice."

"Yeah," Chuy agreed, "and they're competent too. Have you noticed that everywhere we go people know how to serve wine?"

"Not only do they serve the wine," I pitched in, "they know about the wines and the wineries. Whenever we ask them, they give us good advice."

"I like the shopping," said Chuy's date.

We made our way from Ashland to Eugene. It has to be one of the prettiest three-hour rides in America. Rolling hills loaded with timber forests, rivers raging through small canyons, steep climbs followed by winding descents; it was like a scenic roller coaster ride.

We checked into our hotel, and Chuy went to register. He had decided to become a wine educator, and since the annual convention was in Eugene, so were we. Jakelyn's mom and Jake Lorenzo refused to attend a single event, not even the free welcome tasting. We were in Oregon on vacation and that meant finding good places to eat.

For tourists, the right dining experience can pretty much make or break a vacation. In Europe, Jake Lorenzo wanders through towns until he spies the markets. I go into the best looking butcher shop, and ask which restaurants buy their meat. Then I go to the best fish shop, and find which restaurants purchase their fish. Those are my leads, and I follow them, usually to good result.

That doesn't work in America. There are too few fresh fish shops and precious few real butcher shops, most of America preferring to purchase these products in ultra sanitary super market packages. Jake Lorenzo finds that fine, independent bookstores are a great place to start for restaurant recommendations, especially if the staff is young and moonlighting as waitrons.

Once you pick that first restaurant, cozy up to the bar, have a cocktail, and start a conversation about which is the best Thai restaurant in town. Pretty soon you'll have a consensus. We ended up at the Ring of Fire in Eugene. Our waiter was terrific. He knew about the obscure Bogle Petite Sirah on the list for a mere $18. He recommended a delightful Willakenzie Pinot Noir for $28, and when we finished with a rare Madiran from France, he marveled at the tannin when we gave him a glass.

He not only gave us restaurant recommendations, he wrote down the addresses and gave us directions. We used it as our bible, and were not disappointed. Chuy was, however. After a day and a half of wine education, Chuy retired. "Those peoples got no sense of humor. They're too serious all the time. I mean, it's only wine, right Jake?"

"Right you are amigo, what do you say we go out and get a beer?"

"I'm with you carnal, and tell me a joke on the way. I need a laugh."

So Chuy, Jake Lorenzo, and Jakelyn's mom take off for an 11 A.M. beer. As we're leaving the hotel, Jakelyn's mom asks Chuy, "Where's the little woman?"

"She's worn out from shopping, so she's pampering herself with a pedicure."

Jake Lorenzo and Jakelyn's mom stop cold. We stare at Chuy. Chuy stares back at us blankly. Then he starts to grin. Then he bursts out laughing so hard that tears squeeze from one eye.

"This beats the hell out of wine education," laughs Chuy. "Let's get that beer, and then I want a really good three bottle lunch."

DREAMS AND CONSEQUENCES

Truth or Consequences is a strange place. Bleached by New Mexico's high desert sun, the town sold its name to an old time radio show. More recently, tabloids had a field day when a nude woman, wearing only a studded black leather collar, made her barefooted way to the highway. Sordid tales of sexual torture led to arrests, and like an overturned stone uncovering an anthill, exposed a humid, teeming sub-culture of depravity.

But that's not the strangest stuff in Truth or Consequences, not by a long shot.

Between Elephant Butte and the town of Truth or Consequences, just a mile or two farther than a sex slave has to run to escape the clutches of evil, sits the town of Engle. There, in the middle of the Rio Grande Valley, Jake Lorenzo gazed out at more than 60 acres of vineyard. A dream flourishing in this nightmarish place. Rows of chardonnay and pinot noir thriving in some desert oasis.

This dream was too strange for the locals, too strange even for most Americans. This was a foreigner's dream, a second-generation foreign dream at that. The dream saw first light in the Champagne region of France in 1952, where Gilbert Gruet was the first to plant vineyards in Bethon (Marne). "*Mon dieu*," said his French neighbors. "*He ees crazee to plant grapes in zat rockee desert.*" Gilbert's premier bottling of 400 cases came in the mid '50s." His tenacious dedication to quality and perfection created a legacy of beautiful champagnes, until Gruet Champagne now produces 1,000,000 bottles annually in France.

Who knows what it is with the French? Jake Lorenzo thinks it is their ability to focus. They simply refuse to see a reality other than the one they imagine. "*Zoot alor,*" said Gilbert Gruet at a family meeting. "*We must expand eef we are to provide for zee children. You must find your own rockee desert, and make zee dream for yourselves.*"

So in 1984 Laurent Gruet, Farid Himeur, and his wife Nathalie moved to New Mexico and planted their first grapes near Elephant Butte in Southern New Mexico. The first harvest came to fruition in 1987, and in September of 1989 the American contingent of Gruets released the first Gruet Méthode Champenoise Brut and Blanc de Noir. There were 2,000 cases, and it was good. It was better than good. It was terrific, so terrific that they now sell out of an annual production of 35,000 cases. Great sparkling wine, in New Mexico? Who'd have thunk it?

Recently, Jake Lorenzo sat with Laurent and Farid at the beautiful new Gruet Winery in Albuquerque. We were tasting Laurent's initial attempt at producing pinot noir from his New Mexican vineyard. The wine was crisp and varietal, bright with cherry flavors, and rich with just the right balance of oak. I thought, "Pinot Noir in New Mexico?" If anyone can do it, it's these two.

Laurent popped the cork on a bottle of one of their initial 1987 releases. The wine had that gorgeous fat yeasty aroma that only the best sparklers ever think about. There was no hint of oxidation, but rather a crisp, elegant aroma of fresh fruit with the tiniest touch of roasted nuts. The fine beads enlivened the tongue, and the rich flavors washed down leaving a grand aftertaste that refreshed and satisfied at the same time. I complimented Laurent and Farid on the success of their dream.

Farid pointed across the table, "It is our dream, but we could not have done it without the help of our friends from the Wine Patrol."

Indeed, for across the table sat Ken Shoemaker and Doug Diefenthaler, whose New Mexico Wine Patrol is the finest distribution company in all of America. Doug and Ken had more than 20 years of retail and wholesale experience when they started the Wine Patrol in 1989. Fed up with the consolidation of wholesalers, disgusted that fine small wineries were getting no representation, mindful that the wine world was a wonderland of tastes and flavors that went far beyond chardonnay, merlot and cabernet, they bit the financial bullet. They put themselves on the line with a bank, and started the New Mexico Wine Patrol, a distribution company that would specialize in fine small producers.

Talk about a dream. Jake Lorenzo has to tell you, New Mexico is not the place you'd think could revolutionize the distribution business. The entire population of the state is 1.5 million, of which 16% are Native Americans and 45% are Hispanic, not your traditional wine consuming cultures. New Mexico is 47th out of 50 states in per capita income, and 50% of the New Mexico population is at or below federally mandated poverty levels. This is the truth of New Mexico. Doug and Ken now reap the consequences of their actions.

Their idea was to select the finest of the small wineries, to give the best service imaginable, and to educate anyone who would listen to the pleasures of fine wine. They began selling the best wine New Mexico had to offer, which meant Gruet and the small La Viña Winery. Next they selected a tiny block of fine small wineries: Gundlach Bundschu, Qupé, Sanford, Babcock, Ventana, and Diamond Wine Imports. The wines quickly found their niche, especially among the great restaurants of Santa Fe, Taos and Albuquerque.

Ken and Doug called themselves Wine Rangers. Their mission was to select and serve. They tore around the state in the van, making deliveries well into the night. Need something for Sunday? Call Ken and Doug. Need someone to train staff on Thursday night? Call Ken and Doug. Want to acquire a wine no one else has heard of? Call Ken and Doug. If you need it, they'll get it. If you want to learn about it, they'll teach you. You got a wine problem, they've got the answer. The New Mexico Wine Patrol had mounted up, and they were riding hard.

The word got out, and wineries came clamoring for their help. Want Oregon wines? How about Adelsheim, Bethel Heights, Elk Cove, Foris, Sokol Blosser and Willakenzie. California wineries lined up and took a number. Bonny Doon, Calera, Diamond Creek, Dunn, Duckhorn, Kistler, Laurel Glen, Marietta, Coppola, Pahlmeyer, Saintsbury, Seghesio and Spottswoode. They got the best of France and Italy, Australia and Spain. It didn't matter if you were big or small, rich or poor, pompous or down home. If the wine was great, if your heart was in it, if you loved the life, then the Wine Patrol was with you.

As the Wine Patrol prospered, and their dream became reality, they deputized others to help. "We know where the gold is buried," says Ken.

"And the only riches that never tarnish are the currency of friendship," says Doug.

Jake Lorenzo loves dreamers, whether they succeed or not. It's enough just to see them try. Taking a leap of faith, investing in your dreams is a courageous act. Thank God, people try. Sometimes they even succeed. High up on the desert plateau of New Mexico, Gruet Méthode Champenois and the New Mexico Wine Patrol pursue their dreams, and turn them into truth.

Frenchmen and Cowboys. There's no telling the consequences of that.

THE TEQUILA LIFE

On a gentle, balmy night Jakelyn's mom and I sit on the fourth floor terrace of the Fiesta Real Hotel in Tepatitlan, Mexico. We overlook the plaza, dominated by the awe-inspiring cathedral. The plaza is teeming with thousands of people dressed to the nines in Mexican fashion. They are here for the Ferria, the famous, indescribable Ferria de Tepa.

Jakelyn's mom and I are sipping Centinela blanco mixed with Squirt and lime. It's very refreshing, and tastes a whole lot better than it sounds. Chuy is six hours late, and I've realized that we probably won't see him until morning.

Suddenly, explosions rip the night. I'm half out of my chair to get Jakelyn's mom under the table, before I realize the fireworks show has started. Rockets are shot from the church stairs with percussive "whumps" to explode directly overhead in brilliant colored sparks that drift slowly down until they gently pelt our table with debris.

A spectacular twenty minutes of fireworks blister the night. Rickety bamboo towers light up slowly, then spin faster and faster until they scream their high-pitched whistles and burst into a brightly colored tableau of Christ on the Cross, the Chalice, or la Patrona de Tepa. Flaming, screaming carousels of fire spin ever faster until they lift off like spaceships and sail high into the sky to erupt into golden sparkles, while the church bells clang their approval.

We order another round of drinks. I gaze over the smoke filled plaza and marvel at this perfect example of religion at the core of Mexican life. Here on the twelfth day of the fifteen day Ferria de Tepa, where tens of thousands of people suck down tequila and cold beers by the bucketful, where throngs of people come from miles around to eat and dance and listen to the hundreds of mariachi bands, the Church is the home and the sponsor for the celebration. Fireworks are strung from the walls of the cathedral itself, and flame into a glowing finale proclaiming life and religion as integrated parts of the daily Mexican experience.

The party rages throughout the night. Around 3 a.m. we are blasted awake by a mariachi horn section so dynamic, that I check to see if they have somehow crowded into our bathroom. At 5 a.m. sharp, the church bells start ringing. Cannons explode every three seconds for a full five minutes. Nobody, not even Jakelyn's mother, is going to sleep through that. Thinking about it, it occurs to me that the church is saying, "Well, we're glad you had a good time last night, but today is another day. So, come to church to pray, and then get out and do a day's work, feed your family, and then be sure to come to the party again tonight."

We shower, and head down for breakfast where we meet a sheepish Chuy. "Sorry I missed you last night, carnal. I got into an extended conversation with las dos señoritas pouring at the El Tesoro booth, but I talked the chef into making chilaquiles, so we're even. OK?" I don't know if Jakelyn's mom was buying it, but the chilaquiles were pretty good.

Chuy had been hanging out at the tequila pavilion. Much like a wine country event, where each winery sets up a table and pours its wine, here in Mexico they do the same thing with tequila. The booths tend to be more elaborate. Each booth has two beautiful, young Mexican ladies dressed like beauty pageant contestants (even down to the banners extolling Tequila Sauza or Tequila Tapatio instead of Ms. Argentina or Ms. Uruguay.) They pour samples of their various tequilas into little plastic shot glasses, and on occasion extol the virtues of their particular tequila.

It is fascinating to see how much the wine industry and the tequila industry have in common. The key to quality in winemaking is grapes. The key to making fine tequila is agave. Grapes make the best wine when they are fully ripened and mature. Agave makes the best tequila when fully ripened and mature. Grapes are crushed, pressed and fermented. Agave is first baked in ovens (*hornos*) to convert starch to sugar, and then it is crushed, mixed with water and fermented.

Tequila must be made from a specific plant, the blue agave, and the plant must be grown in one of the designated areas, very much like wine appellations. Spirit made from any other type of agave, or spirit made from the blue agave from a non-designated area, cannot be called tequila. Tequila, just like wine, is consumed daily by the local people, and has a direct influence on the cuisine of the region. Neither wine nor tequila comes with a worm in the bottle.

Not only are there great similarities between wine and tequila production, but the tequila industry in 1996 looks very much like the California wine industry of 1976:

- Tequila sales are massively (more than 85%) geared to lower quality bulk tequilas used as cheaper well pours for making margaritas. In the 1970's most wine sales were low-end jugs.
- A few large distilleries (Cuervo and Sauza) dominate the market, in much the same way that Gallo dominated the wine market.
- The Romo family pioneered premium, scientific tequila production with their Herradura line of tequila, in much the same way Robert Mondavi revolutionized the premium wine business.
- Many tiny producers making high quality products have created a whole

new premium category, just as the early premium wineries of the 1970's created a whole new market for wine.

- Excess demand has outrun supply forcing established fine tequila houses to increase production, and creating all sorts of pretenders just in for the fast buck. Think back to the early California wine business.
- Giant corporations are moving in to take investment and/or purchase positions, just as Coca Cola, Seagrams and others did in California.

The parallels between tequila and wine are obvious. What makes tequila unique is that Mexico is the only place that can produce it. They own it—lock, stock, and barrel down to the last blue agave. They don't have any concerns about Californian, Australian, South African or European competition.

Chuy and I are spending a lot of time in Mexico. It is a beautiful, albeit very dusty, country. We would like to see more of a connection between California winemakers and Mexican tequila producers. We advise you to come down and see for yourselves.

If you visit, just remember; when in Mexico, do as the Mexicanos. You can get wine in Mexico, but you probably won't like it, or you'll find it too expensive for what you're getting. So rather than be disappointed, try tequila and squirt with lime, or even tequila and coke with lime. Have it with a plate full of *carnitas*, some roaring hot sauce and some steaming corn *tortillas*. You'll find it a pretty good match.

THE STUFF WITH THE WORM

Sitting in the cab on our way to Teotitlan del Valle, Chuy is beside himself. "You're going to love Oaxaca, Jake. None of that grand tequila factory stuff from Jalisco. These guys are the real deal; small, dedicated, individualistic..."

Jake Lorenzo tries to listen to Chuy's description of mezcal production, but I can't help noticing the look that Jakelyn's mother is giving me. Clearly it says that if we spend the whole week visiting *palenques*, Jake Lorenzo will be one dead detective. Jakelyn's mom is here to shop. She wants pottery, Zapotec rugs, hand-carved wooden *alebrijes*, and jewelry, lots of jewelry.

I've tried to explain that I need to learn about mezcal for the second edition of my book, *The Tequila Lover's Guide to Mexico*. Jakelyn's mother could care less. We're here to buy folk art, and we better get started. Otherwise, she'll be on the next plane out of here on her way to visit Jakelyn and the grandbaby.

We enter the town, and Chuy directs the taxi driver into the first driveway. Pancho Hernandez welcomes us, and starts to show us through his studio. There are piles of hand-spun wool, jars of natural dyes to color the wool, and giant looms made of hand-hewn logs. One room is filled with dozens of gorgeous, brightly colored Zapotec rugs featuring a myriad of geometric designs. Jakelyn's mom is entranced, asking Pancho questions in rapid-fire order. Chuy winks at me. "Hon," I say, "we'll be across the street at the *palenque*. Come on over when you're ready." She waves us off with a disdainful gesture.

I smile at Chuy, "I think this will work out just fine, amigo."

       *   *   *

That week in Oaxaca was a delightful blur. Jakelyn's mother could have opened a retail shop with her purchases. She purchased whole herds of brightly colored wooden antelopes and swarms of carved insects. She bought black pottery from San Bartolo, green pottery from Atzompa, and natural pottery from everywhere else. And rugs, if rugs were magic carpets, we could have flown the entire population of Oaxaca to Sonoma for a long vacation.

Chuy went berserk on the food. We ate each of the seven famous *moles* of Oaxaca. We had squash blossoms and rose petals. We ordered *clayudas*, *tamales*, and *chipotle chile rellenos* that could raise the dead with their smoky heat. We tried grasshoppers as well as insect larvae, and continued with chicken, pork, and beef cooked every way imaginable. We had *carnitas* served by the kilo. We dined on shrimp cocktails, followed by whole fish baked in clay ovens until I thought we'd sprout gills.

We visited dozens of *palenques* and tasted at least 50 different mezcals. I'll tell you something: mezcal is not tequila.

Tequila is a wildly popular, beautifully packaged, uniquely flavored beverage perfectly suited to parties and fun, shots and margaritas. mezcal lurks like a confined older uncle; crusty, unshaven, given to bad breath, but (for those willing to take the time) with a good heart and a grand history.

Tequila is young, hip, likable, daring, and all about façade. If there is an ugly side to tequila, you don't see it until it's too late. With mezcal it's all out there for you to see. Not yin and yang, so much, it's tougher. Mezcal is good *and* bad. Beauty *and* ugliness. Truth *and* lies. Mezcal is smoke and mirrors and mysticism *and* worms for God's sake. Mezcal is in your face, take it or leave it, shit or get off the pot-hard liquor.

Tequila exudes subtle power. It's blue agave complexity with a graceful, complex mouth feel. Mezcal takes *cojones*. Nothing about it is easy. The taste roils with smoke and fire. The smell attacks with volatile aromas redolent of gasoline and creosote. It burns going down. It burns in the stomach. Its flavors assault the mouth, hold on to the taste buds, and seem like they'll never let go. Mezcal is fierce, dangerous, and threatening.

By the way, did I mention that mezcal allows you to commune with your ancestors?

For the most part, Zapotec Indians produce mezcal. The people of Mexico have a tough time economically, but when it comes to economic well being the indigenous people occupy the statistical bottom. Statistics show that 50% are malnourished, 40% have no access to potable water, and one third have no electricity in the home.

Mezcal production is labor intensive. The work is strenuous, sticky, dirty, and demanding. It requires dedication, strength, and intelligence; and it doesn't pay worth a damn. (Sounds a little like the wine business during the 1970's, doesn't it?) So, the work of making mezcal is left to the Zapotecs.

Mezcal retains ceremonial, social, and medicinal significance for the Zapotec people. Mezcal helps digestion when sipped before a meal. Of course, it also helps when sipped after a meal. It will cure the common cold, a cough, arthritis, miscellaneous pains, and headaches. It eases the discomfort of menstruation, the pain of broken bones, and probably the heartbreak of psoriasis. When all else fails, mezcal, along with special herbs provided by a *curandera*, and a strict regimen of prayer can help with cancer, heart disease, and tumors. The Zapotecs are convinced that mezcal creates a unique state of intoxication that opens the doors of communication with the supernatural and their long departed ancestors.

Even the worms, *gusanos*, are credited with special properties. They are powerful aphrodisiacs. Consuming them increases the chances of conceiving male children. They can be used in potions to cure all kinds of illness. They combat curses placed by witches. *Gusanos* can be as powerful as your belief in them, but Jake Lorenzo can assure you of one thing: they don't help the taste of mezcal at all.

I'll tell you something. Jake Lorenzo wants to like mezcal. The people making it work so hard, care so much, and need the money so badly. The production is primitive, conducted in tiny batches, and follows a tradition more than 300 years old. While there's plenty of incredibly bad mezcal out there, several producers are working hard at making excellent product.

Right now Jake Lorenzo is comfortable recommending Del Maestro, Del Maguey and Don Amado. Think of it as a Quixotic endeavor. Get a bottle of mezcal and take your medicine. Visit with your ancestors, and then let me know if you want to buy a Zapotec carpet.

MINISTER OF CULTURE

Jake Lorenzo is on deadline. Normally, I'd have another two weeks to come up with something, but we leave tomorrow for Spain. Since Jakelyn's mother goes semi-hysterical whenever packing for a trip is necessary, this was probably not the most opportune time for her to experiment with lessening her estrogen dose. I discount the occasional screams, and the thuds of things hitting the walls to her crazed, overwrought packing technique. It occurs to me that sitting in my office cranking out a column is good respite.

Our friends react to news of our travels with a mix of delight and resentment. "You dog, I'd love to go to Spain. You're always traveling. Didn't you just get back from Mexico?"

"No," Jake Lorenzo tells them. "We just returned from New Orleans. Mexico was the trip before that."

Most of Jake Lorenzo's friends think I have some outside source of income. It's not true, but I do know a secret. You see, most people work at a job to earn money to do the things they like to do, to buy the things they feel a need to own, and to travel in the style to which they are accustomed.

Jake's secret is that doing the things I like to do *is my job*, and that includes eating good food, drinking good wine, and traveling whenever I get the chance. Because I don't have a normal job, I have lots of time. I can go wherever I choose, whenever an opportunity presents itself. Round trip ticket to Europe pops up for $450, and Jake Lorenzo grabs the passports, waits for Jakelyn's mom to have her packing breakdown, and we're out the door.

Someone calls with free tickets to the Blues Festival in San Francisco, and we've packed a lunch, poured our wine into plastic coke bottles, and are sitting in our folding chairs listening to Blind Willie Somebody wail the blues.

Got an extra ticket to the Giants game? Jake Lorenzo brings both peanuts and sunflower seeds, and I'll buy the first round of beer.

It's rare that I can't get off work, and I have never used up all of my vacation time. I may not have enough money to stay at a $200 a night hotel, but I have the time to find a decent place for $79. (Jake Lorenzo hates to spend more than $10 an hour to sleep.) I may not be able to afford to dine at Restaurant Hot Stuff, but my detective background has trained me to ferret out inexpensive, delicious local joints wherever I may find myself.

Jakelyn's mother and I rarely go out to dinner, but I can manage my way around the stove well enough not to starve, and the wine cellar in my house doesn't work on any mark-up. Clearly food, drink, and good company comprise a job worthy of any private eye. It's hard, but rewarding work. You never know when you will be challenged.

On a recent trip to Mexico we found ourselves in a car driving through the mountains outside Morelia to an avocado farm. Did you know that 60% of the world's avocados are grown in the state of Michoacan, Mexico? (Stuff like that kills Jake Lorenzo.) We walked from the avocado orchard, up the street, to a rustic wooden building with a rusty tin roof. We shuffled across the dirt floor, through the smoke wafting from the wood fire to a rough-hewn wooden table in the back yard. Chickens, pigs, cats, and dogs lazed around the yard. We ordered homemade *chorizo, cecina* (a smoke cured dried pork) *quesadillas, chiles rellenos,* and some of the best beans I've ever tasted. We washed the meal down with a few dozen beers, and some complimentary tequila from the restaurant owner. The bill for eight of us came to $42, more or less the same price as a middle-of-the-road chardonnay in a fancy California restaurant.

One of our hosts at that luncheon had just finished a ten-year stint as the Minister of Culture for the government of Mexico. He was a charming, entertaining man, and later that evening we sat around a roaring fire, sipping good tequila and talking about life.

As usual, the conversation turned to food. I think we were talking about avocados, Michoacan's major crop. From there we started talking about pigs, another big crop for the state. Naturally, the Mexican state raising the most pigs originated *carnitas*, the country's most famous pork dish. According to the Minister of Culture *carnitas* came from Michoacan. Jalisco and Michoacan argue over who developed *birria*, and *tacos* definitely were invented in Mexico City.

"You know, it's strange," said the Minister of Culture, "most cultures have food spread over the world, but not the United States. Italians have pizza and spaghetti. Chinese food can be found in remote places in every country. French food is the technical standard for fine food in every major city. Japanese sushi is worldwide. Mexican *tacos* are everywhere. The French, Spanish, and Italians gave the world fine wine. Mexico has tequila. Russia has vodka, but what has the United States given the world, aside from McDonald's that is?"

Ah, the Minister of Culture had a point, and it was aimed right at Jake Lorenzo's heart.

Here is Jake Lorenzo shivering a bit in the crisp night air and having to speak Spanish. You think it's easy being a raconteur?

I told the Minister of Culture about the cacophony of flavor to be found in a perfectly spiced gumbo. I described the searing, mouth cleansing flavor of green *chile* in New Mexico. I made him hear the crackle of crisp fried chicken in Mississippi. I had his mouth watering for the clean salty brine of Puget Sound oysters.

"*Señor* Lorenzo, said the Minister of Culture, "I am sure that the United States has some wonderful foods. I do not doubt that. In fact, on many an occasion I have experienced such food. My question is about the contribution. What has the United States contributed to the world's culinary stockpile?"

Jake Lorenzo knows when he's being suckered. This man, who for ten years served as Mexico's Minister of Culture, had tons of experience with these esoteric discussions. He had probably discussed artistic values on currency with Ministers of Finance, blabbed about work strategies with Ministers of Labor, debated fungicide application on avocado trees with Ministers of Agriculture. He was setting me up, in a good-natured way, to take a fall.

"*Señor* Minister," I said, "Italy, France, and Spain are thousands of years old, so are China and Japan. Mexico has more than four centuries under its belt. The United States is still a baby. Be patient. Give us some time. I guarantee that we will make our contribution to the culinary arts. In the meantime, you must come visit us in Sonoma. I will take you out for a hamburger that will make you weep. We'll have it with a bottle of California zinfandel and some double fried French fries, which were invented in Belgium by the way."

The Minister of Culture laughed. He offered another glass of tequila. "You know what would be good, my friend?" he said. "A nice juicy hamburger with some of those fresh Vidalia onions."

"That would be good," agreed Jake Lorenzo. "Probably won't happen here tonight."

"Probably not," consoled the Minister of Culture.

Jake Lorenzo reached over and clinked glasses with the Minister of Culture. "Guess we'll be seeing you in Sonoma, amigo."

GARBAGE

Jake Lorenzo loves Friday mornings. Sometime around 5:30 the low rumble of garbage trucks and the hissing of air brakes alerts Jake to pay attention. The sounds get louder as the trucks get closer. And then there is the crash of wine bottles from Jake Lorenzo's weekly consumption splattering into the recycling truck. Better than an alarm clock, I smile, get out of bed, and start my day assured that nobody in Sonoma provides more noise than the weekly bottle dump at Jake Lorenzo's house.

Jake Lorenzo knows this to be true, because the garbage man tells me so when I present him with a magnum of wine each Christmas. "You've got the best bottle garbage in the valley, Mr. Lorenzo," he said. "Nobody else comes close." I feel sorry for my garbage man. I worry about his back. Most weeks, my bottle garbage contains 24 to 48 wine bottles and a couple bottles of tequila and mezcal. He tells me he doesn't mind. "Tell you the truth Mr. Lorenzo, I kinda look forward to it. It's a matter of mutual respect; one professional to another."

I bring up this domestic tale as an entrée into a discussion of perception. People perceive things differently. Jake Lorenzo loves the sound of dozens of exploding wine bottles on a Friday morning, especially when they're mine. Chuy just tosses his wine bottles into the industrial garbage bin behind the Burrito Palace. He derives no pleasure from its dumping. "I gots no time to listen to garbage," he explains. At the opposite end of the spectrum, Iggy Calamari worries about all his bottles. He goes for late night walks on the night before garbage pick up. He distributes his empty wine bottles among his neighbors' trash, so his own trash bin reflects barely a hint of his actual consumption. "I'm a world famous research scientist," he proclaims, "I've got a reputation to uphold."

Imagine using bottle garbage to worry about your image. Jake Lorenzo understands that everyone worries about their image some. It's always helpful to look at things from other points of view when issues are thorny and deep reaching, but it's ridiculous to do something to try to please the perceptions of others. "To thine own self be true" is Jake's motto. If the moral ground isn't high enough on an internal plane, then you're gonna find yourself under water when it rains no matter how you try to please those around you.

Perceptions vary from one community to another. What's considered correct and proper in Sonoma may easily offend someone in, say, New Orleans. After all, you don't see companies doing big business with go-cups in Sonoma. Correct moral judgments in one country may prove abhorrent in another. Imagine a judge in California lopping off the hand of a teenage shoplifter like they do in Iran. Trying to do what other people think is right is a bitch, because other people have different perceptions, and they often have nothing to do with your own.

Last week I had guests in from Mexico. (Jake Lorenzo's house has become a mandatory stop for any tequila producers who happen into Northern California, and last week it was the guys from Espolon.) Espolon is one of the newest tequila producers in Mexico. It's new and modern, so beautifully designed that it won an architectural design award from the state of Jalisco, Mexico. The guy in charge of Espolon's tequila production is Cirilo Oropeza. He has more than 30 years experience producing tequila. Cirilo is a gentleman of quiet confidence. After spending most of his career making tequila for giant corporate producers, this opportunity to ply his skill, knowledge, and imagination for tiny Espolon leaves him breathless with excitement.

Last February, while Chuy and I were rummaging around Jalisco visiting tequila factories, we made the trip to Espolon. After visiting more than 20 tequila factories, Jake Lorenzo had a pretty good idea of what to expect. Talk about perceptions. Espolon is state of the art, without being pretentious (something most California wineries *should* aspire to achieve). Eight out of ten employees are women, in macho Mexico for God's sake. Cirilo walked us through the facility. The best description of his production method is tradition built on a backbone of science. We smelled the candied aromas of the roasting agaves. We watched the mills grind the cooked agave while lab workers took sugar samples. We visited the gleaming distillation room with its stainless steel stills, and spent time in the lab while Cirilo showed us how he uses chromatographic analysis to help analyze his tequila.

Over a simple, delicious carne asada luncheon cooked at the distillery, we tasted Cirilo's tequilas. The Blanco was wondrously rich and oily in the mouth with classic agave aromas and flavors. It immediately escalated to one of Jake Lorenzo's favorite tequilas. Cirilo told us that they only make the Blanco for the American market. "In Mexico, the people drink Reposado tequila, so that's what we make." His Reposado was rich, golden from oak, complex with agave, but alas, a touch too oaky for Jake Lorenzo's taste.

Now that Cirilo is visiting in Sonoma, Jake Lorenzo feels the pleasure of reciprocal hospitality. The first thing I do is set up a tour of the Seguin Moreau production facility. I want Cirilo to learn all about oak barrels. I love the Blanco so much, I keep thinking I'll really like the Reposado if they tone down the oak. Doug and Andy, the brilliant coopers from Scotland greet us upon arrival, and immediately turn Cirilo over to their master cooper Enrique. Enrique, like most of the crew at Seguin Moreau is Mexicano. He gives his tour in Spanish, which puts Cirilo at ease. It's an extensive tour full of detailed explanations and demonstrated techniques. Cirilo is mesmerized, asks loads of questions, and takes in all of the technical information. I can almost see him storing the data in his memory banks for later use. After the tour, we are taken into a room where they give us a chardonnay tasting so we can assess the flavors imparted by different barrels. Cirilo is mightily impressed, and Jake Lorenzo is reassured that the crew at Seguin Moreau will enjoy the Espolon tequila left in appreciation.

We visit some wineries and I show him around the valley. Chuy comes over with Iggy Calamari and that night we have dinner on my porch. We grill some figs from our tree. I serve a cold lamb tongue salad, and I grill some Sonoma County rack of lamb. We drink a lot of good wine. Cirilo enjoys the meal and marvels at the range of wines. I ask him about his perceptions of California and the wine country. "It is beautiful country," he says, "and I am surprised at the dedication of the winemakers. I thought that nobody worked hard in the United States, but I see that they work very hard."

After the meal, we sit on the porch sipping Espolon tequila. Cirilo thanks us for our hospitality. He compliments my cooking and thanks Jakelyn's mom for inviting him to our home. Chuy takes him back to the hotel. I have one more shot of tequila and then go to bed.

The next morning the air brakes hiss, the bottles crash, and I think I hear my garbage man say something. I hope he's commenting on the tequila bottles, and not complaining about back pain.

SIMPLE
PLEASURES

L ife is good.

That's what Jake was thinking as he sat on a secret beach in Mexico. Days filled with warm temperatures, crystal clear oceans, and decent surf. Fresh fish, just minutes from the sea made each meal better than the last. Speaking Spanish from sunrise to sunset was rapidly improving Jake's vocabulary, and devouring a book a day was feeding his mind. Glorious sunshine and the echo of pounding surf soaked into Jake's memory banks cleansing his mind of stress and opening pathways to new visions.

Poverty is a harsh taskmaster, but it does not always overwhelm the human spirit. Our friend Miguel has invited us to his home where we dine on simple, but spectacular tamales prepared by his wife on a wood burning stove. The *masa* is ground by hand, and the *moles* are prepared at home. The green tamales are wrapped in cornhusks, the *mole negro tamales* in banana leaves.

Miguel explains that in Mexico fresh milk is delivered to his house three times a week. Hand-made *tortillas* are delivered daily. He purchases his meats from a neighborhood butcher who slaughters the animals himself after purchasing them from local growers. There are no feed lots, no chemicals, growth enhancers or mad cow's disease. *Chiles*, tomatoes, *tomatillos*, and *cilantro* all come from the home garden. Papayas, mangos, and coconuts grow on nearby trees. Electricity works, and it doesn't cost as much as a bottle of Chateau d'Yquem.

Jake Lorenzo wonders, "What more do you need?"

*   *   *

...Life is good.

That's what Jake was thinking as he drove through Sonoma Valley on a sparkling spring day. Miss Catherine the Whole and the Monsieur himself were in the car along with Jakelyn's mother; best friends on their way to see a movie.

We walk into the theater and take seats after Jakelyn's mother and Miss Catherine wheelbarrow their popcorns down the aisle. The lights dim and we are transported to the wonderfully whimsical world that springs from the twisted minds of the Coen brothers. Oh, brother, what a movie. Gorgeously filmed in a 1937 sepia. Brilliantly acted until the aching poverty of the characters pulsates into your heart. Continuously surprising and inventive until you have to catch your breath at the sheer audacity of it, and the whole thing carried by a soundtrack so deep into Americana that it raises memories we didn't even know we had.

At one point, while the characters sit in a movie theater, which by the way mirrors what we were doing at the time, a character whispers, "Do... not...seek... the... treasure, it... is... an... ambush."

To which another character replies, "We... thought... you... were... a... toad."

"They don't write them like that anymore," says Jake Lorenzo, as we return through Kenwood, the highway clogged with limos jockeying for places among the throngs flooding to the Heart of the Valley Barrel Tasting.

Miss Catherine and Jakelyn's mother take turns giggling as they remember various scenes and lines from the movie, as accountants gleefully count the money clanging into winery cash registers.

Life is good.

That's what winery owners say, while they build their ever more ostentatious palaces, raise, yet again, their astronomical prices, and look down on the flatlanders waiting for the golden calf to come in.

For them, success is selling the family business to some corporate entity for sixteen million, or thirty-nine million, or forty-five million, or roughly the equivalent salary of a mid-range, banjo hitting second baseman.

"Do... not... seek... the... treasure, it... is... an... ambush," advises Jake Lorenzo.

"We... thought... you... were... a... toad," explains it all.

But a kiss of gentle hospitality, a simple shared home cooked meal, a good book on a sandy beach... these things can always turn a frog into a prince.

JAKE LORENZO'S GUIDE TO NEW ORLEANS

Signs. You've got to look for them. This is true for everyone, but it's especially true for Jake Lorenzo, private eye. I'm always watching for signs. In the detective business, you don't want to get old before your time, or you could be dead in no time.

My daughter Jakelyn is now grown up, married and a new mother. That makes Jake Lorenzo a grandpa. In all the time that my kid was growing up and turning into an adult, I never felt I had aged into a different, older generation. True, we had a deal. She could go out with whomever she liked, just so long as she was home by a certain time, and Jake Lorenzo didn't have to converse with the dates when they came to pick her up. My kid didn't dress so different. Her music wasn't so different. She seemed to share a lot of the concerns I had when I was her age.

To tell you the truth I felt a little sorry for Jakelyn and her generation. My generation had raised some hell. Anti-war, drugs, rock and roll, we had ourselves a major generation gap. It seemed as if Jakelyn was still stuck with my generation's values, music and general drug habits. When my parents came to bail me out of jail they would say, "Son we're trying, but we just don't get it." I never had to bail Jakelyn out of jail, not once.

I was sitting in a New Orleans bar after a long day and night of revelry. It was late. Jake was with friends, and we talked about our kids. That's when it hit me. Always look for the signs. Our waitress had a nose ring. There was a tattoo of intertwined flowers around her ankle. The bartender had three visible tattoos and six earrings in his left ear. The chef who had cooked our dinner came in for a drink. He was wearing a do rag, and showing off tattoos. My favorite was two of the Henckel knife figures on his biceps, underneath were the words, "stay sharp."

There *was* a new generation. Jakelyn just wasn't letting me see it. I was, in fact, old and different. There were all kinds of kids under 30 wearing tattoos, piercing parts of their bodies, running studs through their tongues, and doing all kinds of stuff I didn't even know about. I tried, but I just didn't get it. I was elated. I felt a soothing sense of accomplishment. I had finally become part of the "older generation."

New Orleans is the kind of place where you can drink enough for a long enough time to have these revelations. Friends are always asking me to recommend places for them to eat and drink and hear music. I'm sick of writing all this information on cocktail napkins, so I've put it all down for everyone to see. Get your butt to New Orleans and see if this handy guide helps you enjoy yourself.

As for Jake Lorenzo, Jakelyn's come in with her husband, and the baby. They're taking me out for a tattoo. Then we're going to Sears Point Raceway and we're going to jaywalk the track—during a race. I still don't get it, but I'm trying.

THINGS TO DO

It's important to get yourself onto New Orleans time. Stay out late and sleep in. Most action occurs between midnight and 3 a.m. No one else is up early, so get up in time for lunch and you're home free.

1) Take the Zoo Cruise to the zoo. It's a paddle steamboat ride down the Mississippi. Leaves from Canal St. Check out the zoo, cross through it, and take the St. Charles trolley back to town. Good time to stop at Commander's Palace for a meal.

2) Wander around the French Quarter. Keep an open mind. Don't worry, but keep your eyes open. Stay between Bourbon St. and the river, especially at night. Going in the other direction is asking for trouble.

3) Have drinks at Pat O'Brien's, preferably at night. There's a great show to be had watching the tourists get drunk on Hurricanes. Jake's rule in New Orleans bars is to never drink a natural disaster (i.e., hurricanes, tornadoes, blizzards, monsoons etc.) Don't forget that if you return your fancy glass at Pat O'Brien's, you'll get your deposit back.

4) Visit the French Market. It's sort of a creole flea market.

5) Visit Napoleon House for a Pimm's Cup or a Sazerac.

6) Have a real mint julep.

7) Try the aquarium. I hear it rivals the one in Monterey, but I've been to neither.

8) Visit the old K&B Plaza at Lee Circle, 1055 St. Charles Ave. These offices for a major drug store chain house, long since gone out of business, house one of the finest modern art collections in the city. Especially strong in sculpture. Great secret, and highly recommended. Free.

DINING

Eating in New Orleans is a true pleasure, but you've got to leave all your health-conscious, low cholesterol, small portion thinking behind at home. Eat, drink and be merry, for it doesn't get better than this. There are hundreds of terrific restaurants, and I've recommended several, but the best place to learn about dining in New Orleans is from Tom Fitzmorris. He was grown and raised in New Orleans and has been writing and talking about food for 25 years. Check out his website, foodfest.neworleans.com.

TO EAT CHEAP

New Orleans has the best food in America, and you don't have to spend a lot of money to have a great meal. Here are some of my favorite places at bargain prices.

1) **The Praline Connection...**
   542 Frenchman St.

   Terrific, simple creole food for $5-6. Smothered pork chops, turkey necks, red beans and rice, crowder peas. Stark, black and white tile, with real down home food. Terrible wine list. Try beer.

2) **Louisiana Pizza Kitchen...**
   2800 Esplanade

   The best pizza in the quarter, good salads and a decent wine list. Try Jakelyn's favorite, pizza ouvo with an egg in the middle. Located between Decatur and the Flea Market.

3) **Central Grocery...**
   923 Decatur

   Got to try a Muffeletta, and Central Grocery has the very best. Be prepared for the overcrowded space and the somewhat rude service. It's worth it. One muffeletta feeds two. (On Decatur near beginning of French Market.)

4) **Cafe du Monde...**
   800 Decatur

   Jackson Square, on the river side of Decatur. Beignets and coffee, a must for every morning, and a Godsend late at night. (Tables with the napkin holders on their sides are closed.)

5) **Felix's or Acme...**
   Iberville near Bourbon

   The two local places for oysters. Pop in for a few dozen on your way to dinner. Take your oysters at the bar and talk with your shucker.

6) **Mother's...**
   401 Poydras

   HOT POT! is what they yell as they carry the food past you while you wait in line. Funky, informal disorganized with great jambalaya, soft shell crabs, gumbo, etc. Try some "debris", a house specialty.

7) **The Gumbo Shop...**
630 St. Peter

A reasonably priced place to get very good gumbo and other traditional foods, with a very good wine list. Ask to see Guy, and tell him Jake sent you.

8) **Snug Harbor...**
626 Frenchman

Got to have the burger and the baked potato "dressed." A terrific meal for under $10, and they've got a very good wine list. Stay for the music especially if Charmaine Neville's playing.

9) **The Galley...**
2535 Metairie Rd

Seafood is the ticket. Wonderful boiled crawfish and shrimp in season. Fried seafood a specialty, Especially soft-shell crab. Try the onion rings.

10) **Kim Son...**
349 Whitney Ave

Across the river in Gretna. Best Vietnamese in New Orleans. Don't miss salt baked crabs. A hang out for famous New Orleans chefs.

EATING GOOD AND PAYING FOR IT

1) **Commanders Palace**
1403 Washington Ave
504 899-8221

Great and classic. As good as it gets for food and service. Have a drink before you eat and they'll walk you through the kitchen to the garden bar.

2) **Mr. B's**
201 Royal St.
504 523-2078

Always good with great gumbos and inventive touches on their creole dishes. Very good wine by the glass program.

3) **Christian's**
3835 Iberville
504 482-4924

Best soft shell crabs I've ever had. Lamb au poive is sensational. Tables are very close together, and you should tell your waiter you want a leisurely dinner, because the kitchen can crank out the food. Be sure to try a "Skip" for dessert.

4) **Brightsen's**
723 Dante St.
504 861-7610

Great chef, cooks creole rabbit, seafood boudin, delicious fish dishes. Reservations in advance a must.

5) **Gabrielle Restaurant...**
3201 Esplanade Ave
504 948-6233

Very small restaurant with fabulous food. Can't go wrong with any appetizer. Entrées include stuffed quail, homemade boudins, etc. Desserts are terrific, but I've never had room left over to eat one.

6) **Galatoire's...**
209 Bourbon
504 525-2021

My favorite of the old world New Orleans restaurants. No reservations. Ask for Louie (real name Gilbert) as your waiter, and eat whatever he tells you is good. Be sure to tell him I sent you. Careful with wines, often not what's on the list. There's always a line, best time is late afternoon. No shorts allowed, ever.

7) **Andrea's...**   Italian with a creole influence. Salmon and caviar
   3100 19th (Metairie)   pasta, great veal.
   504 834-8583

8) **Bella Luna...**   Gorgeous river views. Horst Pfeiffer will cook you
   914 N. Peters   a great continental meal. Order anything that has
   504 529-1583   caviar in it. Great with any game animal,
                                 especially duck.

9) **Bayonna...**   Susan Spicer's inventive Cajun influenced cuisine.
   430 Dauphine   Try the garlic soup. Likes to work with fresh local
   504 525-4455   products. Outrageous wine prices.

There are lots more. Be sure to go to **Pascal's Manale** (504 895-4877). Tell Bob and Mark that Jake sent you in to try the Barbecued Shrimp po-boy for lunch. Check out the burned shirt in the bar. Ask for Thomas to shuck your oysters, and tell him Jake says hi.

I like **Cafe Giovanni** (504 529-2154) because chef Duke LoCicero is a wild man who can cook. Beautiful presentation and good food. Try the mussels. Beware: portions are huge!

Most recently, a great meal was had at Joanne Clevinger's **Upperline Restaurant** (504 891-9822). Tell her we sent you. **The Pelican Club** (504 523-1504) has great cajun food with a Chinese influence.

To see why New Orleans is the greatest dining city in the world, visit **Clancy's** (504 895-1111), a legendary neighborhood restaurant with terrific soft-shells and some of the best sweetbreads in town.

MUSIC

Pick up Gambit Magazine, free in all the shops. It lists all the clubs and who's playing in them. It gives addresses and phone numbers (for restaurants too.) Shows usually don't start till 9:30-10.

My favorite place to hear music is **Snug Harbor**, 626 Frenchman. It's small, intimate and off the beaten path.

For blues and zydeco I like the **Maple Leaf Bar**, 8316 Oak. **Tipitina's**, 501 Napoleon is the most famous, but it's also big, crowded and uncomfortable.

Mid City Lanes, 4133 S. Carrollton has had some great shows in a bowling alley. The hot place-to-be-seen club is the **House of Blues** at 225 Decatur. In general, stay away from Bourbon St. and go to any clubs that sound interesting.

The best place to hear old time Dixieland style jazz is in the Quarter for the street bands and in some of the large hotels. Look for the guy in the quarter who can play *Stairway to Heaven* on partially filled water glasses.

If *New Orleans Hot Stuff* with Ricky Graham and Becky Allen is playing, you must see it. In fact, if Ricky and Becky are performing in anything, be sure to see it.

FAVORITES

Martini   **Bombay Club**

Tequila Selection   **Vaqueros**

Club   **Snug Harbor**

Poor Boy   **Pascal's Manale** (Shrimp)

Catfish   **Middendorf's**

Crawfish   **Jerry & Catherine's House**

PART IV

MUSING WITH JAKE

Success Is Fleeting

The Court Case

A House Is Not Always a Home

Soothe the Savage Beast

Drunkenness

Dining Out

A Night in Baja Sonoma

The Best

Not for Sale

SUCCESS IS FLEETING

Chuy is pissed. He slams the bottle of Hornitos on the counter, yells, "Pour your own shot, *Señor* Author," and scurries into the kitchen to pick up another order.

The Burrito Palace is jammed. People are actually waiting in line to be seated. At the table behind me, a tourist dips his chip into the bowl of *salsa*, takes a bite and screams. His face flushes purple, his eyes bulge, and he rasps, "Water, ... please, ... water." Chuy grabs the pitcher, snakes his way around the crowded tables, and fills the guy's glass. "I don't make no money on water, gringo, order a beer."

Chuy, never a patient man, is frenzied. I marvel as he deftly negotiates his way around the crowded tables with plates of steaming food intricately stacked up his arm. He serves a table, always remembering who ordered what, pivots to the door and seats the next group just as the bus boy finishes his last swipe of the table top. He plunks down some chips and *salsa*, warns them, "*El mas macho llora aqui*," (The strongest of men cry here), and hurries into the kitchen for the next ready order.

I sadly shake my head, pour a strong shot of Hornitos into my steaming coffee and try to ignore the cacophony of sound. It's my fault, really. If I hadn't written about the Burrito Palace in my book, *Cold Surveillance*, if the food hadn't sounded so delicious, if Chuy had not been presented as such a "colorful" character, this never would have happened.

For two months the Burrito Palace has been mobbed. I had to stop sitting in my regular stool, because people kept coming over for autographs. Local customers complain loudly, and keep adding *habanero chiles* to the *salsa* hoping to drive the tourists off.

Chuy jumps up onto the counter and shouts, "*Bastante! Bastante!*" The crowd ignores him. He smiles at me, our pre-arranged signal. I stand up, pull out the .38 and fire a round into the ceiling. Plaster chips bounce off a buxom blond wearing a tight T-shirt exclaiming "Tequila Hooters" across the chest.

I amble to the door in my best private eye swagger as Chuy announces, "Peoples, finish your food, and then get out. The Burrito Palace is closed." I flip the sign at the door, and then take my position outside, with gun drawn, in case some of the tourists can't read.

It doesn't take long. Maybe twenty minutes. I guess people don't like to lolligag over their meals in the face of gunfire. When the Palace is empty,

Chuy and I toast each other as we start on a 1991 Williams Selyem Rocchioli Pinot Noir. "Gracias, Jake.

"Mañana I'm off to the Caribbean. I got *mucho dinero, mucho vino* and one Hawaiian shirt to last me a month. And when I get back, you better be right. All these damn *touristas* better be gone. I want my business back to normal."

"Don't worry, Chuy. This is America. Celebrity is fleeting."

Not only is celebrity fleeting, celebrity is demeaning.

When Jake Lorenzo walks into a wine shop, in spite of drinking wine every day for more than 20 years, I am overwhelmed by the choices. How could anyone, especially a novice, maneuver his or her way through this wine jungle? What, in fact, actually causes a consumer to purchase a particular bottle of wine? To tell you the truth, I never figured that one out. It's one of the great, unsolved mysteries of Jake Lorenzo's career.

As complicated as a wine shop may be, it's got nothing on a bookstore. Even a small bookstore has hundreds of more books to choose from than a good wine shop has wines. A wine drinker may have to decide whether he wants French or Californian, red or white, pinot noir or zinfandel. But a reader of books has to decide between fiction and non-fiction, travel or business, mystery or sci-fi, classics or modern, hardbound or paperback.

If you think people are reluctant to ask for advice in a wine shop, you should watch them in a bookstore. People become garrulous when talking about wine. The only thing people ask in a bookstore is location. "Where is the quantum physics section?" "Where would I find the original Spanish version of *Like Water for Chocolate?*" Wine is still a diversion. Books delineate the limits of our individual literacy.

Now that Jake Lorenzo has written a book, he spends a lot of time in bookstores trying to sell the damn things. I have been forced to spend time with reporters, trying to interest them in my stories. I have to prove myself attractive to radio hosts, so I can get air time, and encourage people to rush to their nearest bookstore to buy *Cold Surveillance.* For the most part it is a humiliating experience.

Reporters and radio hosts don't give a damn about who you are or what you've got to say. Reporters and radio hosts worry about *their* customers. They want to know if you are a "good story." You're a good story if you're controversial, funny or can in some way provide film footage of anything in flames.

This is a major problem we have in America. People aren't interested in a person until they're convinced that person is somebody important. It's all relative of course, importance exists on a scale. Money skews the scale. If you have enough money, everybody thinks you're important. Celebrity also skews the scale. If you can do something and get recognized for it (i.e. acting, playing baseball, making wine, writing a book,) people will go out of their way to meet you, to be nice to you, to give things to you.

This is asinine, and it smacks of bigotry. We should not relate to people based on their press clippings. If we've lost all else, we should still have the confidence to meet people and decide for ourselves whether or not they are worthwhile. Friendship is far too valuable a commodity to entrust to others.

Hell, Jake Lorenzo wouldn't be surprised if right now Marvin Shanken and Robert Parker were teaming up on a new publication: *The Advocate's People Spectator.*

This is a publication that lists people and assigns them a celebrity value based on a 100 point system. It factors in such elements as recognizability, reputation, humor, estimated value (in dollars), and earning potential. Issues are specialized; one issue covers the entertainment field, another people in the wine business, yet another covers sports figures. Think how handy this will be. Whole groups of people will refuse to associate with anyone scoring less than 90 points.

You think Jake is making this up. Think again. It could happen. In fact, now that they've heard the idea, it's a sure bet. If people are willing to buy their wines based on points, they'd be all too happy to make friends the same way.

More and more it boils down to them and us. I may be stubborn, but I think I'll muddle through on my own. I'll make my own wine choices, with the help of my friendly wine shop owner, even if I have to suffer through the occasional mediocre bottle. And I'll take my friends as I meet them, no matter who they are or what they do. It makes life more interesting.

A
COURT
CASE

"*Carnal*," Chuy was saying, "it's time we did something. This thing has gotten out of hand. I've found a way to change it, and I need the *ayuda* of the *muy famoso* Jake Lorenzo."

"Chuy, I'd like to help, but why me? You know how much I hate being in courtrooms."

"You hate being in courtrooms," Chuy screamed. "Mr. Jake Lorenzo, hot shot private eye, hates being in courtrooms. I'm a goddamned lawyer, and *I* hate being in courtrooms. Why do you think I run this dump of a restaurant? There comes a time, *carnal*, when a man has got to stand up for what is right. Surely, Jake Lorenzo won't refuse his good pal Chuy on something as big as this."

Chuy had me, and he knew it. He refreshed my cup of coffee and then poured in a slug of Hornitos. He did the same to his own cup, took a sip, leaned back, and with a smile that said, "I've got you by the *huevos*," he added, "besides Jake, you've gained 15 to 20 pounds over the last couple of years. *Tal vez*, I am saving your life."

Chuy went into the kitchen to get out some orders. I sat sipping hot coffee thinking about the case. I had to admit Chuy was audacious. His plan had just enough wacky brilliance to slip through our cockamamie legal system. He might actually win.

Chuy, incensed about drunk driving laws, had been looking for a way to challenge them. Chuy feels that .1 or .08 BAC levels are arbitrary, and that enforcement of those artificial levels does very little to combat the real problem with drunk drivers. Evidence shows that the most effective way of dealing with drunk drivers, those who cause accidents, is to give stiff sentences for repeat offenders. Get the continual drunk driver off the streets. Get him into a program if possible, but put him in jail if you have to.

On a more personal level, Chuy pointedly and passionately points out that the police seem to be enforcing the drunk driving laws a lot harder against minorities than against Anglos. In Sonoma Valley, the local *Index Tribune* prints the names of each person stopped for drunk driving. They also print the results of their BAC test. More than half of all the names listed each week are Hispanic, even though they represent less than 15% of the Valley population. Also, more than half the people listed are under .12 BAC

Anyway, Chuy has a plan, and it goes like this: Jake Lorenzo is going to sue the State of California, in a class action suit, don't you know. I will be charging that the State of California is knowingly and selectively passing laws aimed at killing me. They have targeted Jake Lorenzo, (and all the other people who drink in the state,) and they have encouraged me to put on excess weight, (using government funds I might add,) which could have the net effect of killing me off.

Chuy will be pointing to the Department of Motor Vehicles as the main culprit. Every time the DMV sends out a license renewal, it includes a chart explaining that added pounds increase your ability to consume alcohol without going above the state mandated .08 BAC level. In fact it goes so far as to list different weight categories and then tell you how many drinks you can have.

According to Chuy, this is positive, printed evidence that the DMV, (and through them the State of California,) is trying to kill me. "Jake, it makes perfect sense. You are a drinker. You are a driver. You are a law-abiding citizen. The only way for you to morally have a couple of drinks, and then legally drive home is for you to put on added pounds. This, *amigo*, is not *bueno*.

"You will come to the Burrito Palace and eat too many tacos. You will stop exercising. You will sneak *paletas* late at night. You will gain 20-30 pounds, just so you can have one more glass of wine, or one more shot of tequila, and still be legal to drive home. You risk early death, *amigo, muerto temprano*. You risk heart attacks, stroke, bad backs and baldness for all anyone knows. The State is out to kill you, and I'm not going to let them do it."

By now, I'm sure you all wish you had a friend like Chuy.

Not only is Chuy pumped up for this case. He's enlisted the help of Dr. Iggy Calamari for expert testimony. The good Doctor is beside himself with charts, graphs, medical reports and the like. He plans on showing videos in the courtroom of everything from liposuction to open heart surgery to prove that obesity is a killer. According to Dr. Calamari, "When I get through with them, they may want a stiff drink, but they definitely will *not* be going out for dinner."

Then Chuy gets going on his conspiracy theory. It's not just the DMV and the State of California trying to kill me. Hell no, FBI, CIA and foreign governments are out to make mincemeat of Jake Lorenzo. Chuy's got witnesses, tape recordings, and video tapes. He's got tapes of Governor Schwazenegger where he rails against Hispanic immigrants and threatens to cut off schooling and medical care for their children. But when you play those tapes backward you hear the Governor saying, "We've got to kill Lorenzo." True, it's a bit garbled and sounds like something out of the Exorcist, but you can hear it if you want to.

Believe me, it gets worse. If Chuy and Dr. Calamari get their way, O.J. Simpson will have to bribe TV cameras and reporters if he wants to get them out of our courtroom.

Chuy's got integrity though. He's refusing to take any money from the liquor industry, no matter how much they offer. He's refused to market Jake Lorenzo dolls, detective games or overcoats, (although he said I could sell my book *Further Surveillance* during recesses at the trial.) Granted, all the catering for the TV crews, the reporters, and the tabloids will come exclusively from Chuy's Burrito Palace, but that's simple business, and it's the only way to assure that we can get tequila in our morning coffee.

There's no telling how this will all turn out. If it starts us on the road to a more realistic policy regarding drinking and driving in this state, so much the better. If it causes people to think about their rights, and the State's ability to infringe upon them, so much the better. If Chuy's court case forces me to lose my privacy, and my ability to come and go in this life without being harassed by every Tom, Dick and Harry... then there will be one less Hispanic, restaurant owning attorney.

Fortunately for Chuy, Jake Lorenzo is a master of disguise.

A HOUSE IS NOT ALWAYS A HOME

When the fog rolls in causing temperatures to hover just above a spring day in Antarctica, and inexperienced winemakers run about wringing their hands and shrieking at Mother Nature, Jake Lorenzo likes to ponder.

Now that I've crossed the half-century mark, the old body just ain't what it used to be. Truth be told, Jake Lorenzo is lazy. In fact, lazy is one of the prerequisites for being a good detective. If I had any ambition at all, I'd get a real job. Being lazy makes it hard to work for a boss. That's why Jake Lorenzo works for himself. The downside to being self-employed is that usually the benefits suck.

Middle age is upon this world-weary detective. I'm still in pretty good shape, but I am carrying about ten pounds that I don't need, and it's settled in a way so that strangers can see I collected it while sitting at a table. I could only run if it was last call and I needed a drink. That's why Jake Lorenzo went to the doctor.

Actually, I went to the doctor, because after years of miserable benefits from my employer, (me), the bastard went out and got a health plan. Trying to work your way in to see an actual doctor at my HMO is harder than cracking a murder case where the culprit is connected to the powers that be. I've found that unexplained bleeding will usually get you past the register nurse. Tell them you've got blood in your urine, and they'll arrange some doctor's schedule to get you in right away.

Once you get in, and they can't find any blood, introduce yourself, tell them there never was any blood, and let the doctor know what kind of person is sitting on the table. Doctors like it when their patients are honest with them. Jake Lorenzo knows this, because my brother is a doctor.

Honesty is always the best policy, especially when you're talking to a doctor. Lots of people get nervous around doctors. They are reluctant to speak about their bodies and the various malfunctions they might be experiencing. I've never understood this. As far as Jake Lorenzo is concerned, my body is simply a house for my soul. If something is wrong with the house, I try to have it fixed.

Just as with houses, early detection is crucial. Find a bit of dry rot? Rip the stuff out and fix it. It sure as hell isn't going to get better on it's own. Little unexplained lumps or discolored moles are just like dry rot. Rip the stuff out and fix it. It isn't going to get better by itself.

Some people don't live in houses. They live in mansions. So some people make mansions out of their bodies. They scrub them till they sparkle. They festoon them with decorations and jewelry. They tan them and oil them after workouts that make the muscles pop. Some people think they live in temples. You know the type. My body is my temple. They won't put any animal flesh, caffeine, alcohol, or drugs into their pious systems. They graze on wheat grass, slurp carrot juice, and put garlic on everything so it has some flavor.

Jake Lorenzo's house is not a mansion and it's not a temple, but it is lived in and it offers a sense of hospitality. My body is not run down, but it is well used. I'm not saving it for anything. If everything goes perfectly, all my systems will cease functioning on the day I decide to move out.

Some people like to kid themselves. They think they are invincible. Nothing will ever hurt them. I've seen guys having heart attacks, trying to talk business on their cell phones. I've seen people come out of surgery and skip physical therapy to return to their jobs. Jake understands this behavior. This is fear of death. This is denial.

Winemakers do this all the time. They are often terrified by the vagaries of Mother Nature. They can't face the slow death of a stuck fermentation or the dry rot of a bretannomyces infection. Rather than let the natural course rule the day, rather then let the wine make itself; they take out insurance. Use SO_2 at the crusher, and use a bunch of it. Add the SO_2 resistant yeast with plenty of DAP and Superfood. Micro-oxidize the wine to ultimate softness. Clean the wine as soon as possible, hit it with more SO_2 and then filter, filter, filter.

Okay, so they get their wine, and it's not dead, but it is lifeless. What's the point?

Wine, like life or a house, needs to live and breathe. It needs to do things on its own. Only when it gets sick, does it need attention. Most often it will do fine on its own.

Jake Lorenzo sees lots of common ground between doctors and winemakers. They both think that they know what they are doing and you do not. They have time-honored formulas and charts and graphs, and anything out of the norm is bad. With time and patience, they can be trained to do better.

When my new doctor asks Jake Lorenzo if I smoke, I answer, "No." When he asks if I'm taking any medication, I say, "No." When he asks if I use any drugs, I tell him, "No." When he asks me if I drink, I say, "Yes, about a bottle a day, sometimes more."

A good doctor will stop just for the barest hint of a second, trying not to show their shock. Whether it's for the sheer quantity revealed or the surprise of an honest answer, a good doctor will look you in the eye and say something like, "We don't recommend more than a glass or two a day as healthy."

Jake Lorenzo looks that doctor right back in the eye. "Look doc, I try to watch myself, but I like wine with meals, both lunch and dinner. A couple of glasses with each meal and I'm already into a fifth. Company for dinner, I drink more. I think it's healthy for me. I think my body is OK with it. If you find some dry rot, let me know."

And then, so the doctor is not insulted, I give him my gift. "This book is *Further Surveillance*. I wrote it myself. It talks about the life we lead here in the wine country. Try reading it. I think it will give you insight into some of your patients. I know it will give you insight into me."

Usually, the book will do the trick. The doctors start testing my liver once a year, and when the results come back they say, "For Jake Lorenzo, you're doing fine."

Further Surveillance is like a test strip for doctors. If they don't get it after reading the book, I change doctors, until I find one who does. Come to think of it, *Further Surveillance* would probably be a good test strip for winemakers.

SOOTHE THE SAVAGE BEAST

Surveillance is the bottling line of detective work. Boring, mindless, interminable, it still requires expertise and experience. Jake Lorenzo will be truthful. I couldn't be a detective were it not for music.

Sitting in a car for hours, waiting for a suspect to show up, or leave, or have a suspicious guest, would be intolerable if I didn't have my music. They say that music soothes the savage beast. Well, it sure as hell passes the time for a private detective.

I guess a lot of my love for music goes back to my childhood. When I was about 18, my Dad and I were hooked on Bonesville. Bonesville was a funky beer bar on Melrose in Los Angeles. Every Monday night Don Ellis's big band would play. It cost a buck to get in and a buck for a pitcher of beer. Inside the dingy club, Ellis led a screaming 24-piece band through a series of charts delving deeply into weird time signatures. I loved hanging out in that bar, having a few beers with my Dad, while the horn section blasted into the smoky air. I'll never forget leaving the bar each night after the energy and noise from the band overwhelmed the ears. Our sense of hearing almost shut down, and it seemed that we had cotton stuffed in our ears for the ride home. That band never made a record that came close to capturing the passion and fire of those Monday nights at Bonesville

New Orleans is the birthplace for jazz, and lots of other American music. The damp, humid climate mixed with the French, African, and Caribbean influences percolates into a passionate, irresistible sound. My friend and mentor, Jerry Henry, has told me for years that James Booker was *the man*. Crazy, wild, addicted, Booker was a musical genius. I picked up various albums by Booker, but I never got it. I never heard the special quality Jerry described.

One night, while on a particularly arduous surveillance job, I popped in a new James Booker release, *Resurrection of the Bayou Maharajah*. Unbelievable. The piano could have been in the back seat. Transported, I could smell the smoke, hear the tinkle of ice, and even see the wavering of candlelight in the bar. And the music was amazing. Booker was all over the piano, coaxing sounds I'd never heard before. Familiar songs sparkled with frenzied, Caribbean rhythms. For the first time, I got to *hear* James Booker.

A box of cassette tapes had been found. Those tapes documented more than 60 hours of James Booker performances, captured live at the Maple Leaf

Bar. A young record producer for Rounder Records named Scott Billington pored over those tapes, made selections and then painstakingly cleaned up the sound until they captured the music, the passion, and the environment that made James Booker. Like solving a case, Billington had exposed and documented Booker for the genius that he was.

When I finally got home, I listened to *Spiders on the Keys*, the companion CD compiled from the same tapes. I discovered that Scott Billington had produced Booker's last studio album, *James Booker Classified.* I started flipping through my CD's. Beau Jacques and Chris Ardoin, the hottest new Zydeco bands in Louisiana were produced by Scott Billington, so were Geno Delafose and Nathan and the Zydeco Cha Chas. Irma Thomas, Ruth Brown, and nine different Johnny Adams albums; produced by Billington. Duke Robillard, the Nightcrawlers, Davell Crawford, even Tabu Ley Rochereau from Zaire, Africa; all produced by Scott Billington.

Here Jake Lorenzo had collected all sorts of esoteric music, most of which had been produced by the same man. This was a mystery to be solved. I wrote to Scott Billington, explained that I had discovered his link to some of my favorite music, and invited him out for a glass of wine on my next trip to New Orleans. We met, drank some wine, and had a promising afternoon. I gave him my number, and told him to call if he was ever in Northern California.

Last week Scott called. He and Jean were coming up for a visit. Jakelyn's mother was resigned. "We don't know these people, and you've invited these strangers to the house for three days? Jake, honey, you are a piece of work."

We had a great time. Scott and Jean are a wonderful couple. They would hike through the hills during the day, visit wineries in the afternoon, and then we'd cook a nice dinner. They love to eat and they enjoy fine wine. Scott cooked up a fabulous risotto with some lobster mushrooms we found at the local market. We drank lots of wine and spent many the evening listening to music while Scott regaled us with stories about the musicians.

It doesn't sound like much, but wine, food and hospitality go hand in hand. You never know where your interests may lead you. A little wine shared among strangers often encourages a stronger bond. Take a chance, make the first step, and before you know it, wine will introduce you to some new friends. What could be better than that?

DRUNKENESS

Political correctness affects us all. Fashion dictates what we can and can't say at any given time. Yesterday's joke, could be tomorrow's lawsuit. Given the volatility of conversation in today's world, some things are better left unsaid.

On the other hand, Jake Lorenzo is a private eye. It's my job to look behind the curtain, to dig down into the muck, to expose the truth, no matter how horrible or innocuous.

My mailbox gets stuffed on a daily basis with missives from the Wine Institute and various wineries. In the old days I read about new wines, special viticultural methods, and unique fermentation regimens. Later, I collected letters introducing new labels, and bottles with clever printed corks. Recently, I was admonished to fight the "new Prohibitionists," but lately the theme of all this mail is uniformly redundant.

Don't get me wrong, Jake Lorenzo is tickled pink that a couple glasses of wine help your heart. I'm thrilled that wine lowers blood pressure, increases your good cholesterol, protects you from strokes, reduces stress, cures baldness and brightens your teeth. I am reassured that researchers all over the planet dedicate years of their lives, spend millions of dollars, and entice thousands of participants to prove the health benefits of two glasses of wine a day.

Jake Lorenzo wants to know, "Why is the wine industry sending out medical bulletins?"

When Jake Lorenzo goes to his doctor, I go to find out the state of my health. I don't go to ask him for wine recommendations. My brother is a doctor, and I don't ask him which wines he drinks. Hell, I don't even ask *him* about the state of my health. If I want to know about the shape of my arteries, I'll read a medical journal. If wineries want fill my mailbox with paper, at least write about wine. Better yet, just send samples, and I'll make my own conclusions.

Not only that, but Jake Lorenzo would like to know what's up with this two glasses a day? At Jake's house, we *break* more than two glasses a day. What about two bottles a day? That's closer to the truth.

There's so much medical research being pumped out that wine sometimes sounds like medicine. It's not. One of the best things about wine is that it gets you high. Here, you see, we approach the verboten subject. Every once in a while, Jake Lorenzo thinks it's a good idea to get ripped, to tie one on, to drink yourself into oblivion.

You know what Jake Lorenzo likes? I like a long slow drunk with friends over a good meal. I like the way the whole evening ebbs and flows around the conversation, the courses of food, and the bottles of wine.

The pop of the first champagne cork excites Jake Lorenzo. Sitting on the porch sampling a few simple tidbits gets the conversation going. Sipping on a crisp, but not tart champagne prefaces a lovely and lively evening.

Moving to the table, we observe with simple pleasure the hand-woven placemats created by Jakelyn's mother, and comment on the blood-red dahlias from the garden. We open a bottle of spicy, dry gewurztraminer that perfectly sets off a smoked sea bass served with a *picante* cilantro sauce. The talk centers on food, with occasional stories and some good time laughter surrounding the table.

Next let's try a couple bottles of pinot noir. Repartee rears its welcome head. The wine bottles get passed back and forth across the table. Guests settle into a comfortable relaxation, as a small course of Cajun boudin is served. Conversation veers to New Orleans, music and memorable meals. The laughter gets louder and more regular. The wine bottles empty.

I send the guests down to the cellar to choose wine for the main course: leg of lamb with garden fresh potatoes. They return with a zinfandel and a cabernet sauvignon. We enjoy the meal, sipping at the wines. As we eat and drink, it occurs to Jake Lorenzo that life doesn't get any better than this. I remark on it, and in our sweetly juiced frame of mind, we embark on a high-flying discussion of life, its meaning, and its mystery. We are in perfect intellectual sync, appreciative of each other's cogent observations and delighted by each hilarious riposte.

We refresh our palates with a crisp tomato salad. Voices get louder, more brazen. The laughter becomes more frequent. We make another trip to the cellar, and return with some old treasure to sip with the plate of cheeses. Talk centers around children, generations, and the future. Speech slurs a bit. Sometimes stories go on for too long. Inevitably someone loses his train of thought.

We offer coffee, a bit of desert. "Just so you can soak up the port." Having moved into the house, we listen to some quiet jazz, sated physically and mentally. Jakelyn's mother and I insist that our guests make a choice: spend the night, or opt for a cab. We call the cab, "Be right there, Jake," says Bert the driver.

When they've gone. I help Jakelyn's mom rinse and stack the dishes. Then I pour a small shot of fine Añejo tequila and sit in the living room reflecting on the evening. I stagger a bit as I turn off the lights, and head for bed. I laugh, knowing I'll have a headache in the morning. If only we could remember whatever the hell we were talking about tonight, we would solve many of the world's problems.

"Jake," I say to myself, "you'll never remember. You'll have to invite them again."

DINING OUT

Jake Lorenzo is well into the third bottle of pinot noir for the evening. "I'll tell you what gets me, Chuy. I often see things that are obvious. I mean they're right there for everyone to see, but no one sees them except me. I can't understand how people miss the obvious."

"I know what you mean, *carnal*, and you don't have to be no detective to figure things out."

"Exactly," says Jake, " I'll give you a silly example. We are working on a book about tequila, and people keep asking us about mezcal. Here's a product that actually has a dead, segmented worm in the bottle, and people still insist on drinking it. I mean, those same people would race to the nearest lawyer's office to start proceedings if they ever found one of those *gusanos* in a bottle of Coca Cola."

"*Es la verdad*, Jake, and on the *otro mano*, looking at the positive side, you get a cold so you go to the *farmacia* for some medicine. There's all kinds of pills, sprays, and liquids, but the choice is obvious."

"*Claro*, Chuy. You go for the Nyquill every time."

"*Sí*, you got to buy any medicine that comes with its own shot glass."

*   *   *

Some nights are just like that. You're sitting around with a couple of friends. You're relaxed. You have some good food. The bottles seem to empty of their own volition. Pretty soon, you've become very philosophical about all kinds of things that make sense at the time, but never seem to stand up in the bright light of the next day.

When Jakelyn's mom and I are on our own, when we're in some new part of town looking for a restaurant, the first rule is, "No more than 50 seats." I mean there are all kinds of great restaurants with hundreds of seats, and all the right people drink overpriced wines and cocktails while they wait in line hoping to get a table. I much prefer to take a chance on a tiny establishment, especially if it is owner run.

Walk by a new restaurant, and most people look at the menu to make their decision. That's why restaurants put their menus up in the window. Jake Lorenzo says forget the menu. If a restaurant looks inviting, ask to see the wine list.

These days a lot of restaurants have what I call a "screw you" wine list. Nothing is under $20, and nothing you'd be willing to drink is available for under $30, with prices escalating quickly to $60 bottles. These lists are usually made up in equal parts of esoteric stuff from unheard of regions in recently emerging third world countries, and all those wines so hip that no one can ever get them, even though they score 98 in whatever publication happens to be lying on the table in your doctor's office at the time.

Give these restaurants credit, they let you know what you're in for from the outset. If you stay when presented a "screw you" wine list, then you deserve everything you get. The proper response is to rise from the table quietly, explain to the waitperson that you just remembered you have children who need a college education, and gently stroll out to a different restaurant.

Faced with a fine wine list, one that has been selected with an eye toward compatibility rather than profitability, you are on the first stage toward a delightful evening. A fine wine list should contain simple charms like dry gewurztraminer, perhaps a crisp Chablis, a fresh dry rose, a wide variety of reds, and a pleasant selection of sparklers. It can be dotted with some more expensive treasures, if the mark up is reasonable, but the list must have decent wines at all price levels. As a customer, I want to see evidence that the restaurateur has made his own decisions, searched out some real values, and has passed those values on to his customers. It is obvious to Jake Lorenzo that the restaurateur, who takes the time to build a fine wine list, probably takes the same care when he selects his fish, produce and meat.

A. J. Liebling, the great glutton and writer, pointed out that expertise in dining and drinking comes from the experience of weighing various delights against their cost. If you are rich, or on an expense account all of your life, then you will eat and drink what others say is good, and you will never learn for yourself. Go to a restaurant with a limited amount of cash and you face serious decisions that will only enhance your gustatory knowledge.

Let's say for example that a restaurant has a lovely and lively pinot noir for $22 and a fine French Corton for a reasonable $38. That same restaurant also offers a simple lamb stew for $10, but it has venison, which you'd love to try for $20. Jake Lorenzo has to decide between having the venison with the pinot noir, or indulging in the Corton with the stew. I can learn for myself whether or not the lively pinot noir stands up to the venison. I can discover whether or not a fine Burgundy can turn a simple dish into a glorious one. The rich person will likely have the venison *and* the Corton. He has not had to make an economic choice, and he is therefore unlikely to learn the charms of a lively pinot noir. Nor will he readily discover the power of a good stew.

Restaurants are fraught with opportunities for embarrassment, Jake says push on, and be sure to maintain a sense of humor. As much as I like to drink wine, I've always thought this thing of smelling a cork was ridiculous. All too often a cork reeks of mold or ethyl acetate, but the wine in the bottle is fine. I've come up with the perfect procedure. When some snooty waitron presents you with a cork, take it carefully in your hands. Hold an end of the cork into the gentle flame dancing above that romantic candle on your table. When the cork is well charred, blow on it gently to cool, and then draw a mustache or sideburns or even a goatee on your waitron. It will definitely get their attention.

The issue of corkage is another terrible restaurant affliction. Jake always orders at least one bottle of wine from the list. After that I figure there should be no corkage charges for anything I've brought from my own cellar. Unless the waitron is a complete ass, I always invite them to sample each of the wines we're having. I consider it an additional tip, and each of us must help educate others to the joys of wine. If waitrons tell me that the management doesn't allow them to sample wines when offered by the guests, I commiserate with the waitron, and don't come back. I figure if a restaurant owner is too dumb to let the customers pay for educating their staff, then there's no hope for them whatsoever.

The finish of a meal is always interesting to observe. To Jake Lorenzo's trained eye, there is a fascination in watching the dessert junkies. There are large groups of diners who would gladly forego a fine meal, so long as they can dive into a delicious dessert. I don't understand this aberration, but I have great respect for it. Dessert lovers, relish their treats with such loving devotion. I can't imagine a better finish to a fine meal than to have Jake Lorenzo sipping a fine glass of port, while the dessert lover across the table rhapsodizes over the delicate nuances of chocolate, fudge, cream and marzipan tucked into a paper thin buttery crust. Jake Lorenzo drinks his dessert, but I get real pleasure watching others eat theirs.

Finally, when the check comes, be a mench. Spending money for a fine meal and some good wine is a generous act. It's good for the economy. Your cash contribution keeps restaurants open. It keeps meat, fish and produce suppliers in operation. It pays for printing wine lists, menus, buying napkins, silverware, and toilet paper. Your tips help busboys support their families, and they help waitrons support their various late night habits. So pay the bill with a smile, tip large, and leave with the satisfaction that you've done your part in support of culinary excellence.

A NIGHT IN BAJA SONOMA

Chuy and Jake Lorenzo hunch down in their winter coats against the November night chill. Never mind that we've had a fine four-course dinner, and along with Jakelyn's mother have already sucked down four bottles of wine. "I can't believe we're going to eat after that meal, amigo," says Chuy.

"It was four hours ago Chuy, and you know the rule."

"*Sí, sí*, I know your damn rule. 'If you don't eat, you die,' and I could use something, you know what I mean."

Jake smiles, "Absolutely *carnal*, I know exactly what you mean."

The two friends brave the Highway 12 crossing, which even at this 1 a.m. hour can be harrowing, and we walk the block to *Taqueria La Bamba*.

The truck stands like a beacon, a chain of exposed light bulbs hanging from the temporary awning. The harsh glare of bulbs promises some warmth, but our breath is still frosty in the night air. The two picnic tables are half full, and three people are ahead of us in line, but all in all it's not a bad wait.

Chuy tells Jake, "You are one lucky *gringo*, *amigo*. Only you could build a house one block away from the best *taco* wagon in the valley."

"You call it luck," responds Jake, "I call it preparation."

"What are you gonna get," asks Chuy.

"I always order the *suadero*, even though they NEVER have it. But if one night they actually have it, I want to see what it is."

"It's a Mexican custom, Jake. Every place has to have a specialty, but if you have it all the time, then it's not special. It's like trying to get *pupusas* from the *Antojitos Tavo* wagon down the street. They're always on the menu, but never when you order them."

"Yeah," Jake agrees, "but you know my favorite, *torta de pierna*. It's got to be one of the greatest sandwiches ever made. Jakelyn's mother loves the *tostada de carne asada*. Then we have to try some of the specials."

"Here's one we've got to try," exclaims Chuy. "I've never seen this on a menu before. They're selling *tostadas de cueritos*."

"You're kidding me," says Jake, "that's the soft fried pork skin isn't it."

"*Exactamente amigo*, we'll have to check it out."

Jake orders, "*Hay suadero esta noche?*"

Inside the truck there is laughter, "*No, señor, esta noche no tenemos, losiento.*"

Jake orders a *torta*, a *tostada*, the *tostada de cueritos*, and six *tacos*. The bill comes to $17. They wait for their order, and soon get handed two bags.

"*No olvide la salsa*," says Chuy, and inside the wagon they hustle out three plastic cups of their green *salsa*.

Behind them the crowd has intensified. Six workers in chef's pants and white coats peruse the hand painted sign on the truck that serves as a menu. Three young guys, tattooed and pierced with brightly colored hair, stumble a bit as they order a half-dozen tacos each. Two carloads pull up, and what appears to be a wedding party climbs out.

Jake and Chuy deftly work their way through the crowd, and cross Highway 12 again. "This place does some business," says Jake.

"And it's 1:30 in the morning," adds Chuy, "you've got to love that."
In Jake's house, we unwrap our treasure. Each order sits on a paper plate wrapped in tin foil. The tin foil lids come off. The six *tacos* rest on tiny 3" corn *tortillas*. "I got three *lenguas*, and three *cabezas*," Jake announces.

"Tongue and beef cheeks," says Jakelyn's mom. "Eat your heart out Loretta Keller."

The *torta* comes on a gorgeously toasted soft bun filled with piles of juicy pork roast, lettuce, salsa, *crema*, and *jalapeños*. The *tostada* completely covers the plate piled high with tasty grilled steak, lettuce, cheese and *salsa*. Each of the plates is adorned with grilled green onions, radishes, and pickled *jalapeños*.

The star of the show is the *tostada de cueritos*. "Check this out," marvels Chuy. The *tostada* sits on a giant rectangular piece of *chicharron* (fried pork skin). It is covered with lettuce, *crema*, and dozens of pieces of tender *cueritos* that have been marinated in lime juice and chili powder. The whole thing is then slathered with red, hot sauce.

"I've never seen anything like this," proclaims Chuy.

"Of course not," says Jake, "your family's from Jalisco. Most of the food from these taco wagons comes from Michoacan."

We sit sharing this delicious food while we drink a homemade tempranillo. When we finish, Jakelyn's mom says, "We've got to find a *taco* wagon from Oaxaca so we can get a regular fix of *mole*."

Chuy walks in from the wine cellar with a bottle of Centinela Añejo. "That's it Jake. We need to go on a quest. Let's go to every *taco* wagon in the wine country. Let's taste every single dish, and then let's write a book about it."

We sip the tequila and outline our book. At the time it seems like a very good idea.

* * *

The next morning Jake Lorenzo gets up early. Chuy is still asleep in the guest room. Jakelyn's mother, a legendary sleeper, won't be up before noon. I sit at the computer and start looking up some history and statistics.

Long ago Sonoma Valley used to be part of the Mexican territories. General Mariano Vallejo was in charge of the area. On June 14, 1846 thirty-three armed American settlers demanded that Vallejo surrender to them. Vallejo invited the three leaders into his home for breakfast and wine.

"Breakfast and wine," thinks Jake Lorenzo, "what a wonderful heritage we have in Sonoma. (I don't bother to check, but I bet somewhere in past history over in Napa it's "Brunch with a banker.")

Vallejo knew which side of his toast was buttered and gave the revolutionaries his support. In thanks, they threw him in jail. (Vallejo eventually returned to Sonoma where he served as a delegate to the California Constitutional Convention, and later became a State Senator.) This revolt came to be known as the Bear Flag Revolt, because of the rough hewn bear flag carried by these thirty-three men having breakfast and wine with General Vallejo. It also led to California leaving Mexico and eventually becoming a state.

Not much happened for the next 156 years. Sonoma stayed a sleepy little agricultural town. The local people lived in small adobe huts and raised their meager crops. Yeah .... right! Does the word monoculture strike a chord? See the hundreds of ostentatious wineries draped with their sparkling stainless steel tanks and surrounded by their manicured vineyard moats. (But Jake Lorenzo has railed too long and hard on that subject.)

This is about something subtler, and infinitely more interesting, especially if you are hungry at 1 a.m. According to the 2000 Census, half of the nation's 28.4 million foreign-born residents were born in Latin America. Mexico accounts for more than half of them, and of those born in Mexico 50% live in Texas and California. Foreign-born residents born in Mexico have the least education, the fewest managerial and professional jobs, and the lowest average income of all other foreign-born residents. They have the largest families and earn the least amount of money. They are our plumbers and electricians, our carpenters and painters, our waiters and waitresses. And, of course they are our vineyard workers.

156 years after Vallejo's wine breakfast, Mexico has reclaimed Sonoma. The two mile stretch of Highway 12 from Mountain Avenue (the first stoplight as you enter the valley from the north) to Verano Avenue (where the McDonald's is) looks and feels more like Mexico than California. People are out in droves...*walking*. Imagine people walking in California. Men walk the streets selling ice cream from pushcarts, strawberries from hand trucks, and balloons from thin wooden rods.

There are five *taco* wagons operating in that two-mile stretch of highway. Ninety percent of the food is terrific and all of it is inexpensive. Jake Lorenzo says you should stop by and try it, or try one near you. Wine Country *taco* wagons are easier to find than PG&E trucks, and they're much more efficient. One thing, better bring your own wine. They aren't on to that, yet.

THE BEST

Chuy is in Jake Lorenzo's wine cellar perusing the bottles. He meanders through the pinot noirs, tempted by a 1996 Casa Carneros and a 1990 Beaune. He moves through the syrahs, passes the small merlot section, and stops at the zins. Chuy selects a 1993 Guerrilla Vino zin from Toovey vineyard, and a 1986 Gundlach Bundschu to be decanted for later. Back in Jake's gleaming new kitchen, Chuy decants the Bundschu zin. "I love your attitude about wine, Jake. You always have people go in there and pick whatever they want."

Jake Lorenzo flames a pan of foie gras with Maison Surrenne cognac, waits for the flames to die, and then pours the liquid into a waiting pan of spiced apples. "I think it's a sign of hospitality, and usually people will pick stuff I forget that I have."

"Don't you worry that people will pick your best wines?"

"Hell, Chuy, how are they going to pick the best wines? How would they know? I mean they might pick the most expensive wines, or the most famous ones, or even the ones that won the most medals, but the only way we're going to know the quality of the wine is to pull the cork and taste."

Chuy pours some of the Toovey zin for Jakelyn's mom, then fills Jake's glass and his own. "Umm," says Jakelyn's mom. "I like this. It's unctuous and full of fruit."

"It is delicious," agrees Chuy, "what's the story with this wine, Jake."

Jake sips from his glass. "It's the last great year from Cathy Toovey's vineyard. By 1994 she had built a second story on her house and a barn behind the vineyard, so I think the vines just couldn't get enough sun and air circulation. We really couldn't get the grapes ripe anymore."

"It's spectacular," says Chuy. "How much of this is around?"

Jake smiles, "The vineyard produced six cases. I gave Cathy four. I think we've got four or five bottles left."

"Six cases!" exclaimed Chuy. "What happened to the rest of it."

"That's all there was," explained Jake. "It's not really a vineyard. Back in the eighties, Tracy took some cuttings from the old Pagani vineyard and planted them in his backyard. 30 or 40 of the vines took, and we made this wine out of them."

"This could be one of the finest zins I've ever had," says Chuy. "What if this turns into the best zin ever made with another year or two of aging? What will you think about having drunk this bottle now?"

Jake laughs, "First of all, I'd think how good it tasted tonight, especially with the foie gras and apples. Then I'd remember how much the three of us enjoyed it. Finally, I'd know that it can't turn into the best zin ever, because no such thing exists."

"Sure it can," argues Chuy. "There's a best of everything. There's a best kind of car, a best dishwasher, and a best hot sauce. There's got to be a best zinfandel. Hell, that's the whole point of tastings and wine competitions."

"It's all bogus," insists Jake. "Every person and every thing has different good points that lead to excellence, but there's no such thing as best."

Jakelyn's mom picks up the dishes. "It's awfully early in the night for this kind of discussion. I'll whip up my pasta now." She admonishes Jake, "Be done with this conversation when the food hits the table."

Jake ignores the comment, pours more zin into their glasses and continues. "There's no such thing as the best, Chuy. I've never understood why so many people insist on this kind of quantification. It only makes you unhappy."

"It doesn't make me unhappy, *amigo*. Chuy Palacios makes the best *burritos* in California. Hands down. No argument. End of *la cuenta*, and that makes me happy."

"Your *burritos* make a lot of us happy," Jake agrees. "But if you make the best *burrito* in all of California, how come you drag me over to the Ranch House once or twice a year for one of their shrimp *burritos*? You seem to enjoy the hell out of those."

"It's simple, Jake. Chuy's Burrito Palace doesn't make shrimp *burritos*. We make plenty of different *burritos*, but not shrimp. So when I get a craving, I go to the Ranch House."

"That's my point exactly," Jake says pounding the table. "There's no single best *burrito*, there's a myriad of different great *burritos* that qualify as the best, depending on your individual mood on any given day. You don't make *burritos* out of turtle meat either, but remember those *caguama* burritos we had in Puerto Escondido."

"*Madre de Dios*," exclaims Chuy, "those were divine. I'm starting to see your point, Jake. There is not a best wine because one day you might want pinot noir and another day you might want cabernet."

"Right, and one night you might want something young and vibrant, and another time you might want something old and refined. It's one of the great pleasures of Mother Nature, my friend. Mother Nature is all about variety. Think about how many different kinds of roses there are. They come in different shapes and sizes, with different colors and aromas. Then they mutate into mixed colors and blends, long-stem and short-stem and wild with almost no stem. You could spend a lifetime studying roses, and never get to see all of them.

"But Mother Nature doesn't stop there. Roses aren't enough. There are daisies and daffodils, violets, gardenias, orchids, and so many other types of flowers that we'd never be able to name them all. Surely, there is no best flower."

"Ah, but Jake," suggests Chuy, "maybe there are so many different flowers because Mother Nature is looking for the best one. She just hasn't found it yet. What about that, amigo?"

"I suppose that could be the case," Jake ponders, "but I don't choose to live in that kind of world. Too many people spend all of their lives aspiring to the best. They want the best car, or the best house, or the best wine. If they can't tell which is the best, then they go for the most expensive figuring that cost must indicate quality. They spend so much time looking for the best thing, that they are miserable worrying about not finding it"

"Well, we don't have to worry about that Jake. Between us we don't have enough money to buy the most expensive anything. We're lucky that the best things in life are free, right *amigo*?

"Absolutely, Chuy, my friend." Jake refills the glasses. "And you know what's nice about there being no best of anything?"

"I can figure it out," says Chuy. "If there's no best thing, then whatever you've got that you're enjoying is a pretty good alternative. You can take pleasure in the moment."

"Right you are, *amigo*, and here comes Jakelyn's mom with a truly great pasta."

"And after this, we'll have an incredible old zin," chimes in Chuy.

"And maybe," inserts Jakelyn's mom, "we could have a really good discussion about which drapes to put on the windows."

"Now there's a discussion that we could have," laughs Jake.

"That could be the best discussion ever," agrees Chuy.

NOT FOR SALE

Awise man learns from the mistakes of others. A smart man learns from his own mistakes, and some damn fools just won't learn. I'm not sure where that puts Jake Lorenzo.

Remember Jake's concept of voting with your dollars? I thought that was a good idea. Spending money locally, supporting those people whose vision excites you, is a wonderful way of assuring that they succeed. If they succeed, they remain in your life, which makes your life better.

I now have a corollary of voting with your dollars. Jake Lorenzo says that we have to find like-minded people and introduce ourselves. That way we create a support network. We need to let people know when and where we find art, intelligence, and compassion, so our friends can take a look for themselves.

Last year, while in New Orleans, we went to see a Zephyr game at the new ballpark. The Zephyrs are a triple A baseball club currently owned by the Houston Astros. The park is gorgeous, state-of-the-art, with good hot dogs. Before each game, a group of Little Leaguers takes the field with the baseball players. Starting players stand with a kid on either side, and they all have their caps over their hearts while the *Star Spangled Banner* plays.

After the game, every kid in the park is invited to run the bases. Hundreds of children line up in the stands and pour out to first base. They run like hell around the bases and all the way home. As Jake Lorenzo watched the unending line of children scurry around the bases, I thought, "This is terrific. This is what baseball should be. This is what it was for me when I was a kid."

Then I look at modern professional baseball players crying about being disrespected. I see them ditch teams for fatter contracts. Give me a break. We should be ashamed of ourselves.

A friend of mine is a record producer. Last year he made a record with Johnny Adams. Johnny Adams is an incredible singer. His voice is rich and pure. He can hold, sustain, twist and play with individual notes like no one else that I've ever heard. Johnny Adams has made dozens of albums. My friend produced eight or ten of them.

In 1998 they made *Man of My Word*. It's Johnny Adam's last album. He had cancer when he made the record. Everyone knew this would be his last record. They created an album so driven by talent and simple emotion that it makes you cry. Every note, every phrase, every guitar riff and horn chorus is perfect. Johnny did what he does. The "Tan Canary" sang his whole life in just under an hour. Jake Lorenzo says it's art, pure and simple.

Man of My Word won't sell 10,000 units. *The Titanic* soundtrack sold millions. Give me a break. We should be ashamed of ourselves.

Walter Mosley is a great writer. Jake Lorenzo knows his detectives, and Mosley's Easy Rawlings is a good one. Sometime, somewhere, Walter Mosely wrote a script. Somehow, someway, it got made into a movie. It's not a perfect movie, but it takes us into a world that we don't often get to see. It introduces a black man, Laurence Fishburne, trying to live a moral life, and shows how he deals with an older mentor and a young boy. In short, he's a wise man, a smart man, and a damn fool all rolled into one. No wonder Jake Lorenzo likes him. The picture has the misleading, miserable title of *Always Outmanned, Always Outgunned*.

Jake says you should dig for it at your local video store. It's worth the search. Then I look at movies like *Dumb and Dumber* and *Armageddon*. More than $200 million earned for that stuff? Give me a break. We should be ashamed of ourselves.

Jake Lorenzo sits in his new house in Sonoma. Two ex-winemakers sit at the table with him. They are the founders of Underground Winemakers, a non-commercial organization of winemakers producing wines that are not for sale. The woman had worked at several high-profile wineries, done some consulting, and then got out.

"The business ate me up," she said. "I became a winemaker because it gave me a chance to test myself against Mother Nature. I loved that part, but when the emphasis changed from making the finest wine to making wine that the critics liked, I lost my desire.

At first I thought I didn't want to make wine anymore. Then I realized I had to *make* wine, I just didn't want to be in the *business* of wine."

She poured two of her wines. Exquisite. The first was a blend of sauvignon blanc and semillon. It was crisp, dry and steely like a Graves. The second was chardonnay, but tasted of Chablis, full of crisp mineral complexity with none of that commercial buttery malolactic syrup. She found these wonderful grapes in the Santa Lucia Highlands of Monterey. She makes one 60-gallon barrel of each wine in her home. The wine is not for sale, but she gave me a couple of bottles.

The man makes pinot noir. It's an obsession. "I was a professional winemaker for almost 20 years. I've got to say that I loved every minute of it. But I learned an important lesson being a winemaker. Every attempt to achieve something is gained at the cost of something else. To gain fruitiness, we must sacrifice complexity. To gain buttery texture, we must sacrifice tart, crispness. You can't have it both ways. You must choose.

"It seems that everyone chose money. It's like a formula: grow more grapes per acre, make the wines softer and more ready to drink, use newer oak barrels, continually make more wine and raise prices annually. I don't think you can maximize profits, and maintain the joy of winemaking."

We tasted four different pinot noirs from four different vineyards. Each was distinctive, complex, extracted and aromatic with a wonderful velveteen texture in the mouth. Those four wines were some of the finest California pinot noirs Jake Lorenzo had ever tasted. The man gave me a few bottles.

My editor said, "Give me a break. You should be ashamed of yourself. You're going to write about wines that no one can buy? What's the point of that?"

Jake Lorenzo thought a minute, then I said, "Magazines write about rich people starting up extravagant wineries all the time. Those people charge fortunes for their wines, and only other rich people can afford to buy them. It seems to me that winemakers working from a genuine love of the winemaking process, who produce tiny amounts of exquisite wines, and then give those wines to their friends, are a valid story. What makes overpriced wines sold to your wealthy friends for exorbitant prices a better story than fantastic wines given to your friends for free? What makes commerce a better story than friendship?"

"Maybe you're right," he said. "We'll run the story, but do you think you could get me a couple of bottles of that pinot noir? I'd like to get a few of the whites too."

"I told you," answers Jake, "the wines aren't for sale."

"C'mon," pleads the editor, "I'll even pay up to $50 per bottle if I have to."

"Your money's no good here," I explain. "These wines are not for sale, at any price."

"All right, you bastard," he screams. "If they're as good as you say, I'll pay up to $100 per bottle."

"They're still not for sale," smiles Jake, "but I would have been a fool to let you have them for $50, wouldn't I?"

"Aw, c'mon Jake, it's your old pal the editor talking here…"

Like I said, some damn fools just won't learn.

PART V

THE WINE INDUSTRY

Tribute

Bum's Rush

Greed and the American Way

The Cellar Rat Ball

Interrogation

Bigger Is Not Always Better

A Wild Hair Idea

TRIBUTE

Nowadays, million-dollar winery showplaces are a dime a dozen. In 1955 there was only one. Owned by Ambassador James Zellerbach and named after his wife Hanna, Hanzell Winery was the first crown jewel of California wine. Sitting atop the Southernmost point of the mountain range that forms the Eastern wall of Sonoma Valley, Hanzell offers visitors breathtaking views of Sonoma Valley that stretch all the way to San Francisco.

Hanzell has always been a magical place. Ambassador Zellerbach, a prime architect of the Marshall Plan after World War II, wanted to make wines that would compete in quality with the finest French Burgundy. He purchased his property in Sonoma, and Italian immigrants living in the Bay Area insisted on planting his vineyards, as a way of thanking him for his support of Europe after the war. Talk about good karma.

Ambassador Zellerbach hired 32-year-old Brad Webb to be his first winemaker. Webb had some previous experience making wine and vermouth at Gallo, but more than anything, Webb wanted to make wine using the scientific method.

He remembered that first interview with Zellerbach; "I kept going over and over the point that I wanted to make wine using the scientific method. I wasn't interested in racking by the light of the moon, although people were making good wines that way, but I was interested in the scientific approach. I kept pounding that point."

Finally, Zellerbach said, "Mr. Webb, I've gotten your point very clearly. I employ many chemists in my paper business. I know exactly how they work, and that's the way I want us to go about making wine."

Webb got the job all right, and a good thing for the California wine business. Brad's "scientific approach" made Hanzell the first winery to use stainless steel tanks and French oak barrels in California. He developed inert gas technology, using nitrogen to prevent oxidation. Brad discovered that the secret to malolactic fermentation was building the inoculation in the juice, instead of the wine, and he determined the best way to culture the organisms.

Brad was a scientist through and through, "I just can't understand why you should not operate knowing what you're doing, especially if it's something you can quantify. I think if you're not doing anything else, you should be measuring something. It's silly when you can control some variable, not to control it."

As Brad got older, and his battles with Parkinson's Disease got fiercer, he even invented a machine he called the Twitchometer. He would take the medicines prescribed by his doctors, and then measure their effects on his shaking with the machine. Then he would present his meticulous notes to the doctors.

Webb was an honorable man. He felt a sense of indebtedness to his country, and was a member of the Air Force Reserve for most of his life. He raised a family. He helped found an entire industry. He gave of himself freely and often. Brad told me he sometimes felt guilty working as a winemaker. "Yeast works 168 hours per week, and I only work 50 to 60 hours per week. It seems the least a winemaker could do would be to work as hard as the yeast."

*   *   *

Certain people are just special. Somehow, you just feel better knowing that they're around, even if you don't see them very often. Molly Sessions was like that for me. Molly's husband, Bob, is Hanzell's current winemaker.

More than anything, Molly made me laugh. I never had the sense that Molly was trying to be funny, but she had that ability to describe everyday occurrences in such extraordinary ways that I couldn't help but laugh. Molly could always cut to the chase, you just were never quite sure of who was chasing whom.

In the old days when there were less than a dozen wineries in Sonoma Valley, we'd have these horrible business meetings. Various winery owners would get in a lather about some serious issue. Debate would rage. Accusations and counter charges would fly. Just when things would start to get out of control, Molly would say something to Bob or to me, (I always tried to sit next to Molly), and we would both start laughing out loud so uncontrollably that the debate would disappear. Molly Sessions was like a corkscrew for bottles of goodwill.

Molly never succumbed to the celebrity of the wine business. She knew the business too well. For a quarter of a century, she worked beside her husband running the business of Hanzell Winery. She knew about the broken pumps, the dead tractor motors, the sore backs from lifting barrels, and the dead ache of exhaustion. Hundreds, even thousands of times, she poured Hanzell wines across a table, and listened to taster's comments. Never once did I hear her complain or put on airs.

She had a deep wisdom that comes with common sense and a good heart. I didn't always understand what Molly was trying to tell me, but I never left an encounter without feeling the better for it.

Brad Webb and Molly Sessions died within five months of each other; Brad in September as harvest started, Molly in January having seen the year 2000. The first crown jewel of California wine is in serious mourning. Brad and Molly have enriched the lives of countless people. Jake Lorenzo hopes you, too, were among them.

BUM'S RUSH

"Listen, Jake. Can I call you Jake? Right, so like I'm telling you, we've got the whole deal. We're not playing around here."

Jake Lorenzo watches as the man spreads out some drawings on the counter of Chuy's Burrito Palace. The man is dressed casually, if casual can cost thousands of dollars. Italian slacks, silk shirt, Spanish leather shoes. The Rolex, and the tasteful diamond pendant hanging from the gold chain like a ripe grape, merely decorate the ensemble. "Money" is what it says, and the guy can talk. Boy, can he talk.

"Jake, look what I'm showing you here. These are the plans for the winery. We've already got the property. Well, actually we're in escrow, but it closes pretty soon. Beautiful. Just beautiful. You're gonna love it. High up in the hills overlooking Sonoma Valley. Some days you can sit up there in the bright sunshine looking down on the fog filling the valley, like some gigantic cotton cloud that's flooded paradise.

"See the plans. The winery is modeled after Chateau Petrus. We're importing Italian marble for the floors. The windows will be stained glass representations of the grape harvest. Place will look like a goddam church.

"Everything's state of the art. Nothing but the best. We got a crusher that's so gentle the grapes don't even know they're being squeezed. Our press cycles are programmed down to seconds to give the winemaker absolute control. We buy our yeast directly from Berlex labs, where they've cloned special yeast cultures to our specifications. No one else can use them, because we've paid for exclusivity. Believe me, it wasn't cheap, but in today's market you've got to be a step ahead. You know what I mean, Jake?"

"Know what he means, Jake?" asks Chuy, as he pours another Negro Modelo for me. Chuy makes a lewd masturbatory gesture directed toward the man who is bent over rummaging through a hand-tooled alligator brief case.

"Look at this," he says, extracting a tall, smoky colored burgundy bottle. "This is the finest glass in the world. Hand blown in Lucca, Italy. Same company that makes those crystal grappa bottles. We're not crapping around here, Jake. Everything is first rate. If it's not the best, then we're not interested.

"But it's not just smoke and mirrors here. We're not some rich group of dreamers who don't know what we're doing. It's not all marketing here. We aren't just building a showplace winery, and using fancy bottles, and decorating the package with a glorious label. By the way, did I tell you we've got

Chuck House doing the label? He's the best in the business, but we're not using that Francophile, jokey style that Randall Grahm's got him into over at Bonny Doon. Hell no! We've got more class than that. Chuck's going to design the most elegant wine label that has ever graced a wine bottle. It will knock you out. The label alone will sell ten thousand cases.

"But like I was saying, it's not smoke and mirrors here. We're after quality. That's why we hire the best, most experienced people. Know who our consultant is going to be. Go ahead, take a guess. You'll never guess. Andre Tcheleschieff, that's who's going to be our consultant. Of course, we haven't actually signed him yet, but our people are talking with his people."

"Lots of luck, Señor," laughs Chuy. "Tcheleschieff died years ago. I think that pretty much means he's retired."

"See, that's what I'm talking about," says the man, "we're not rookies here. We've got back up plans for whatever the contingency. We find out that Andre can't make the gig, we're ready. We probably should go with someone younger anyway. That's why we're talking with Helen Turley. You don't come any hotter than that. She could make wine out of stones."

Jake Lorenzo is not amused. He thinks to himself, "I could be doing something important like playing hearts on the computer. I don't need to listen to any more of this crap." Trying to be polite, Jake says, "Listen, I think you're really onto something here. Thanks for sharing this beautiful dream with Chuy and me. We wish you the best of luck. We really do, but I've got to be going."

"C'mon Jake. You can't kid a kidder. You're too shrewd for me. I know, sometimes I go on too long, but I'm so pumped. I'm so into the vision of this thing. Sometimes I can't help myself.

"Let's cut to the chase. You can see that we're serious. We're only interested in the best. When it comes to this detective business, the best is Jake Lorenzo. We're not crazy, Jake. We know it's not enough to have the best winery, and the best equipment, and the best consultants. There's more to it than that, man. We've got to get some grapes. I mean, you can't make wine unless you've got some grapes, right? That's where you come in Jake. We want to hire you to find the grapes. We want the best grapes in California. Price is no object. We don't care what the variety is, just so long as they are the best.

"And, Jake, I don't have to tell ya, time is of the essence here. I mean crush will probably start in a week or two. We can't have this great winery, without the grapes. So we came to the man. Jake Lorenzo, the best in the business. We'll pay your fee. We'll cover all expenses. We'll give you a bonus."

He holds out his hand. "What do you say, Jake? Are you with us, pal?"

Jake Lorenzo rises from the stool gracefully. He grasps the man's outstretched hand, and with lightning speed twists it behind the man's back. Using the arm like a rudder, Jake propels the man straight through the Burrito

Palace and out the door. The bewildered man stands outside the restaurant as Chuy hands him the hand-tooled alligator brief case with the hand blown Italian bottle and the expensive drawings.

"Sorry Señor, Jake says he don't share your dream. For him, it's sort of a nightmare. Comprendo amigo?"

Chuy walks back into the Burrito Palace. Jake is sitting at the counter sipping on the bottle of El Tesoro Añejo. Chuy pats his friend on the back. "Where the hell do these people come from," asks Chuy. "That's the third one this week."

"I don't know," answers Jake. "But I think I know how the Indians felt when the settlers made their push. There's more of them than there are of us." Jake glares into his glass, as he pours more tequila. "One thing for sure, those bastard's ain't putting me on no reservation."

GREED AND THE AMERICAN WAY

Jake Lorenzo knows how to work a table. To my mind, there's nothing better then eating a fine meal, drinking a few good bottles and enjoying the company of friends at table. It has been Jake Lorenzo's experience that most true aficionados of wine happen to be fair to middlin' cooks, with a talent for hospitality. I suppose truly appreciating a fine wine is so dependent upon good food that real wine lovers prefer to leave nothing to chance.

Jakelyn's mother and I entertain two or three times a week. Cooking a meal and dining with friends is one of Jake's great pleasures. Sadly, having a relaxed dining experience at home is a lost art in modern America. People prefer to entertain in restaurants, or worse, to serve foods prepared by industrial chefs at their local, fancy supermarket.

It's a national tragedy. There is something so comforting about sharing home, hearth and the dinner table. It is that intangible mystery against which no restaurant can compete. In fact, whenever Jake dines at a local establishment, and finds the food delicious, I find my way into the kitchen and invite the chef over for a meal. Initially, of course, the chef thinks I'm blowing smoke up his griddle. Sooner or later, the tenacity of my continued invitations wears him down, or he hears from others, and before you know it, Chef is sitting at my table asking for seconds.

Lest we forget, Sonoma County is a major producer of fine agricultural products. I source food for my table the way good wineries source grapes. I search out dedicated growers who exhibit care and love for their produce. In so doing, I make great long lasting friendships. Excellent oysters, mussels, clams and abalone are available for the taking just an hour away, and traveling to the ocean always makes for a great day. There is no finer lamb than Sonoma lamb. Not only is fine duck available, but we also are blessed with Sonoma Foie Gras. My neighbor raises rabbits and another raises squab. All of northern California is a breeding ground for wonderful wild mushrooms. Cheeses are made from virtually any animal from which you can squeeze some milk whether it is cow, sheep or goat. Produce of any type, color, shape or size is available from local producers.

As any winemaker knows, great grapes produce great wines. The same is true with food. Start with fresh, well-raised, undiluted food products, and the finished meal will be delicious.

Jake sees you all shaking your heads. You're thinking, "This is obvious. So what?" Glad you asked. Jake will tell you what. This whole winemaking-grape-growing thing is getting out of hand. Greed is running rampant in the wine business, from farm to bottle, and Jake Lorenzo is starting to get pissed off.

It doesn't take an experienced, toughened private detective like Jake Lorenzo to see what's going on. Any tourist, even if he's barreling down the highway at 60 miles per hour with a good heat on from an afternoon of tasting, can see the myriad of trellising systems. He can see the quadruple and octuple and muchotuple arms of grapevines extending into their adjustable wire, multiple lyred, quagmired wire systems. Tourists take note of the continued light green tendril growth as growers "feed 'em the water." Even with the grapes fully colored, ready to harvest, our speeding tourist can see the sun glistening through the water drops as the grower continues his drip regimen.

To tell the truth, Jake Lorenzo doesn't see much difference between current modern viticulture and hen-house raised chicken. Don't poultry processors try to convince us that keeping chickens penned up, feeding them all sorts of hormones, confusing them with bright lights until they don't know day from night, is the way to make the best, highest quality chicken meat for the discerning consumer. "Chicken feathers!" says Jake Lorenzo. They're not making better chickens. They're making more money.

If all this modern technology works, why doesn't the chicken taste like chicken? Chicken has become so tasteless that people compare it to everything from frog legs to rattlesnake. You want to know what a real chicken tastes like, buy one from a local grower, or better yet get one from your own backyard.

Grape growers with all their talk of water management, canopy management, fertilization techniques, trellising systems and vigor, vigor, vigor, are simply growing more grapes. They've managed to raise yields and maintain numbers. The grapes look fine in the lab, but the grapes have no flavor. Grapes with no flavor make wines with no flavor. Grape growers talk about improving quality, but lots of them are more concerned with improving quantity. They're not growing better grapes. They're growing more money.

I know that things are tough out there for grape growers. Phylloxera is wreaking havoc. I know it's expensive to plant or replant. The competition is huge, and it's getting worse. Just look at the miles and miles of new vineyards going in everywhere from Santa Barbara to Eureka. I know that it is boom time in the grape business, that prices are at an all time high, that the smart businessman makes a killing while he can.

Is that what we've become?

Jake Lorenzo says remember how you got here. Remember when your vineyards were orchards, when apples, pears and prunes covered the land.

Remember when selling the stuff to the canneries meant you could pull a heavier crop, when you could shave a little quality, when low prices forced you to compromise here and there. Remember what happened to that industry.

America has a great propensity for following the leader. It is easy to get on a roll and drag along millions of followers. Americans like to do what is hip, cool or current. But it is all part of the cycle. Creative, independent thinkers start with a dream. They turn that dream into a small success. Businessmen take that success, and turn it into major profits. Marketing people take the product and make it more palatable to a larger segment of the population to make more profits. Little by little, we get something so innocuous, so generic, so tasteless, that nobody remembers why they are using it. Fortunately, America also has a great tradition of individuality. There are pioneers who don't give a damn about money. They get involved in things for the challenge of it. They need to make a living, but they recognize other satisfactions. They see the charm or living a rural life style in a modern world. They recognize the life enhancing qualities of a fine meal shared at a family table.

Sooner or later, America will always reinvent herself. It's happened with beer, where after Budweiser, Coors and Miller killed off all the small breweries, their own indifference and tasteless products reinvented the microbrewery boom that continues to sweep the nation. It happened in agriculture, where the sweet, syrupy preservative added to canned pears and apples, reinvented glorious fresh produce of all types and varieties in our grocery markets.

It will happen in wine making as well. If our industry continues in its quest to produce the least offensive wine to all people, it will find itself outsold by small producers selling to the chosen few. If grape growers continue to enhance quantity instead of quality, then they will soon find themselves selling for less than upstart neighbors who value intense varietal character and demand a premium price for it. If wineries continue to charge all that the market will bear, then they are destined to be replaced on the shelves by a myriad of charming, inexpensive wines from France, Australia, and South America.

Jake Lorenzo says make your own choice. Go for the money, or make great wine. Personally, I think making great wine is the high road. That's always the road I take. I like the view.

THE CELLAR RAT BALL

Way back when Jake Lorenzo first moved to Sonoma Valley in 1977, there were plenty of people making wine, but there was no real "wine business." The big annual event was the Sonoma County Harvest Festival. Awards Night was the one night during harvest that every cellar rat got a few hours off. They would drive into Santa Rosa, go to the cavernous Vet's Memorial building and have a hokey little tasting. A table would display some chunks of cheese and some French bread, and 20-25 wineries would pour samples of their wine. The people working the tables were cellar rats, their hands black from handling grapes, their eyes sunken from lack of sleep. The event was open to the public, but very few of them were willing to brave the raucous cellar rats.

Cellar rats would often abandon their tables to circulate around the room drinking the other wines. This was no tasting; this was drinking pure and simple. Eventually, the crowd would move to folding chairs in front of the stage and the awards would be announced. As best as I can recall from those early years, Dick Arrowood won virtually every award. Of course, the cellar rats heckled him unmercifully, and cheered like crazy whenever anyone else won anything. One year I think the biggest ovation went to the Sonoma French Bakery for their award winning bread.

By 1980, Awards Night had moved over to the County Fairgrounds, and pretty quickly it became a public relations showcase for the Sonoma County wine industry. Ticket prices went up, people started dressing in tuxedos and gowns, press people got all the complimentary tickets that used to go to the cellar rats. Before you knew it, the cellar rats had disappeared from their own Awards Night.

Concurrent to this development with Awards Night, a similar thing was happening at the individual wineries. It was a time-honored tradition that the end of harvest was marked with harvest parties. Usually a pig was roasted. Sometimes a deer was slow cooked in the Mexican birria style, but somehow each winery marked the end of each harvest for its working people, the cellar rats. Once again, these parties were loads of fun. Winery owners couldn't resist inviting growers, and then press people, and then important buyers. Before you knew it, the cellar rats had disappeared from their own harvest parties.

In general, Jake Lorenzo is not a big fan of nostalgia. I am, on the other hand, a big fan of history, especially the history of the common working person. By 1988, I realized that nothing was being done for the cellar rats. Cellar rats could no longer afford to go to their own awards night. They were pretty much ignored at their own harvest parties. It was all they could do to scrape together enough money to buy the very wines that they had made, even with winery discounts. Something had to be done.

I got together with Chuy, and we invented The Cellar Rat Ball. The first ball was held in Sonoma at the Vet's building across from the police station. I hired Norton Buffalo to play. We provided beer, wine, Sonoma sausages, cheese and French bread. The cost was $7.50, but if your hands were stained black from working with grapes, or you came wearing rubber boots then you got in for free. It was a wild, rollicking good time party. Cellar rats from all over Sonoma county were swapping crush stories, having some good food and drinking a lot of beer and wine.

1989 was the vintage from Hell. Rain, and lots of it, had made for a miserable crush. Hours piled up; there were no days off. Cellar rats struggled with moldy white grapes, but somehow produced decent, drinkable wines. By the time the Cellar Rat Ball rolled around, the cellar rats were ready to party. More than 250 cellar rats showed up. Poking fun at the Awards Night crowd, many of the cellar rats wore tuxedo jackets with Bermudas and rubber boots. Female cellar rats wore prom dresses stylishly set off against their rubber boots. It was a wild, hard drinking night that left Chuy and Jake a little shaken when we got to thinking of liability problems.

We offered the Cellar Rat Ball to the local winery associations. We were willing to put on the event, but we needed help with the liability angle. There were no takers, and the Cellar Rat Ball disappeared.

The wine business boomed in the 1990's. Most wineries doubled their work crews. By 1995 hundreds of cellar rats were working in Sonoma Valley. Old timers spoke fondly of the Cellar Rat Ball and wondered if it would ever return. New cellar rats were eager to sample a bit of wine industry history. Finally, Rob Larman, owner of Rob's Rib Shack, a funky barbecue restaurant next to a driving range, agreed to host the Ball.

Last night was the 1996 Cellar Rat Ball, and it was glorious. About 200 cellar rats showed up. The admission price was $15 and included all the food you could eat, all the Gordon Biersch beer and Sonoma Valley wine you could drink and the chance to hit a bucket of balls at the old driving range. As soon as the first keg was emptied, a spontaneous beer keg tossing contest was initiated.

Everywhere you went cellar rats were drinking, having a good time, and swapping crush stories. One cellar rat told how his winery had held their harvest party, and whoever cleaned up the trash threw it into the pile of stems from harvest. Evidently smoldering embers from the left over charcoal ignited the mountains of stems into a blazing inferno that required the presence of three fire trucks.

Another cellar rat told a story about a grape delivery. She described how a trucker parked at the top of the crush pad, dropped one trailer loaded with grapes, and then got ready to back the other trailer down to the crusher. Evidently, the trucker forgot to set the brake on the first trailer. It started rolling down the hill, picking up speed until it rammed into the must pump, ripping it out of the ground and separating it from the must lines. Cellar rats were laughing with tears coming out of their eyes as she described their attempts to piece things back together to continue crushing grapes.

Another story revealed an inexperienced cellar rat had left an air line running into a bladder press until the bladder burst spraying grapes into every nook and cranny of the winery. Another cellar rat told how they had dealt with a miserable part time worker. They got the worker to climb into a wine tank to scrub it down. They closed up the tank, locking the worker inside, and then started filling the tank with water until the water level was three inches higher than his boot tops. Plenty of cellar rats thought that was a great idea and filed it away for next year.

Plans for next year's ball are already being made. We're trying to get life-size cardboard cut outs of various winery owners to put out on the driving range. That way the cellar rats will have something to shoot for.

The point of all this is that the wine industry too often forgets its own. It's the cellar rats, the vineyard workers and the tasting room crews who make this whole thing possible. We need to do something exclusively for them. We need to provide a place where workers can share the misery that is harvest and the joys that make the wine business. It is this verbal history that will be the legacy of the wine business. The Cellar Rat Ball is just the ticket. Throw one in your neighborhood next year. Your cellar rats will love you for it.

INTERROGATION

There's an art to interrogation. When Jake Lorenzo speaks of interrogation, I'm not talking about torture. I'm not talking about tying some poor soul to a chair and submitting them to all types of physical and psychological abuse. No, what I'm talking about is the intelligent use of conversation to extract information.

Cops are artists at interrogation. When they put you in the precinct sweatbox to ask you a few questions, they are at home on their own turf. They are masters of persuasion, of confusion, of timing. They can turn things around until you don't know up from down, right from wrong, Chablis from Burgundy. Spend a few hours with cops in a small room, and they'll have you confessing to crimes you never knew existed.

That's why I tell Jakelyn's mom, "If you ever get taken in by cops, get a lawyer. Never answer cop questions. They've got an agenda, and that agenda is not helping you out of a sticky situation."

You're probably thinking, "What does this have to do with wine? In fact, given Jake's propensity to wander when choosing his subject matter, what does this have to do with life?" You're probably thinking, "I'll never interrogate anybody, and hopefully I'll never be in a situation where I am being interrogated."

Well, Jake Lorenzo has news for you. This isn't like high school trigonometry, which has limited use outside of the academic realm. Once you realize that interrogation is the intelligent use of conversation to extract information, you understand that interrogation is the interview. We have all been interviewed: there are job interviews, medical histories, and eyewitness reports.

Most of us are familiar with job interviews. If you are in the wine business, especially in a management position, you've probably spent plenty of your time interviewing people. If you actually own a winery, then you know that hiring the right winemaker is crucial to the success of your business. Interrogation is an art form that you should learn. It can save you a lot of grief later on.

As Jake Lorenzo sees it, there are just two things required when interviewing someone for a winemaking job. First, you want to make sure the person has enthusiasm. No one can make decent wine if they aren't enthusiastic. They need to have plenty of energy and drive if they are going to get through crush. Simple questions that elicit their interests will usually let you know about their enthusiasm.

Second, there's the question, and the question is, "What's your favorite sport?"

If your candidate answers mountain biking, lose him. If she answers marathon running, tell her to set her running shoes on the exit road. If they answer football, punt them over to some other winery.

There's only one sport for true winemakers... baseball.

Baseball is the perfect metaphor for winemaking. If a winemaker doesn't understand the nuances of baseball, then there's no way that winemaker can navigate the travails Mother Nature will place in front of them.

Think about it. Baseball starts with spring training, a rite of renewal where everyone has hope, confidence, and a chance for a great year. Spring training even coincides with bud break. At exactly the same time your favorite ballplayer is stretching his muscles and shaking out the vestiges of the off season, your grapevines are popping their buds and shaking off the chill of winter.

The regular season is a long drawn out affair, but every day counts. One single game can make the difference at the end of the season, but the simple regularity of things; the "every dayness" of it can lull you into inattention. It's the same in the vineyard. From bud break to harvest is six months. Nature seems to take care of itself, but before you know it mildew is cropping up, or mites, or some root louse.

A winemaker is to the crew, what a manager is to his team. There are no recipes. There is no magic formula. Intuition, experience and luck all play a part. A good manager can deflect media attention away from his team, and he can deflate pressure buildup among his players. A good winemaker must do the same with his cellar rats. Both managers and winemakers need to get everyone working together for the common good. That's teamwork, and it leads to great results.

Baseball is all about continuous reappraisal of data, and then making spontaneous decisions based on that data. A hitter must adjust his thinking according to the count. Fielders must position themselves according to the pitches thrown to the batter. In winemaking, especially during harvest, things change from minute to minute. A winemaker must be relaxed enough to assess these ever-changing situations, and attentive enough to make the right call.

The playoffs and the World Series occur during harvest. At the exact time that winemakers are under the gun, baseball plays out for us under its greatest tension. Winemakers think in terms of vintages. 1999 was late, but the weather held. 1997 was the huge crop. 1994 was the great year. Baseball fans remember the turning points. They remember the ball rolling through Buckner's legs or the kid reaching for the fly ball and turning it into a home run.

Baseball, like winemaking is pastoral, timeless, and ongoing. It consists of a myriad of details, most unknown and unseen by the public, all of which contribute to success. In both instances, as soon as you finish one great season, you've got to start over, and try to make it happen again.

There's only one question, and that question is, "What's your favorite sport."

There's only one answer, and that answer is "Baseball."

On the other hand, I guess you could answer, "Drinking wine at a baseball game."

BIGGER IS NOT ALWAYS BETTER

Perspective is an odd thing. It's never the same for any two people. To Jake Lorenzo, Chuy Palacios is average height. To Kobe Bryant, Chuy's a short guy starting to bald on top. To Jake Lorenzo, Chuy's hot sauce is just right. To Kobe Bryant, it's a burning chili torture that swells his tonsils, and makes him fall down clutching his throat like P.J. Carlissimo after a Latrell Sprewell attack. To most basketball fans, Kobe Bryant is the best young player in the NBA. To Chuy, he's just another tourist who talks big, but can't handle *picante*.

Jake Lorenzo has his own unique perspective. Generally, I like things small. I prefer small oysters that you can slurp down rather than the really large ones you have to chew. I enjoy dining on several small delicious courses, rather than trying to stuff down an entrée that requires a hydraulic lift to be settled on the table. I am fond of well-behaved medium-sized dogs as opposed to 140-pound monsters that jump up on you, knock you to the ground, and lick your face like you were a bowl of gravy.

Don't get me wrong. Jake Lorenzo likes lots of big things. Mountains should be big, and capped with snow and pine trees. I like big planes when we're traveling so the turbulence doesn't toss us around like bungee jumpers off the Golden Gate Bridge. Grand Canyon is a much more interesting crack in the ground than the trench they keep digging in Highway 12 each summer to screw up the traffic at the height of tourist season in Sonoma Valley.

When it comes to events, I don't really care how big they are. I'm more concerned with how crowded they feel. Jake Lorenzo and Jakelyn's mother went to Jazz Fest in New Orleans for 12 consecutive years. For a long time it was our favorite festival. The food booths sold delicious portions of Creole specialties for $3. About 25,000 people would comfortably roam the usually muddy grounds. Various stages would feature local acts like Bois Sec (all of whom were over 70), the Bluerunners (who were just starting out), and classic Big Easy singers like Lillian Boutté or Leah Chase. Headliners would be the Neville Brothers, Doctor John, The Meters, or Fats Domino. All in all, it was a New Orleans thing.

Nowadays Jazz Fest crams 50-80,000 people a day into the Fairgrounds. Food prices have doubled. The emphasis on local acts has given way to giant national acts like Jimmy Buffet, Al Green, Bob Dylan, and Phish. Jake Lorenzo agrees that all of these acts are great (well, I'm not sure about Phish), but what happened to New Orleans? I'm sure the managers of Jazz Fest love the higher prices, the crowds, and the prestige of the big acts. From their perspective it's a much more successful event. More than anything, they love the money rolling into the coffers. "Some of it goes to charity, you know."

Jazz Fest keeps getting bigger, and hundreds of thousands of people love it enough to keep going, but from Jake Lorenzo's perspective it has become a bloated, over-crowded, pretentious party. I have a better time at the smaller, much more local French Quarter Fest. In fact, New Orleans by the Bay right here at Shoreline Amphitheater every June offers more of what I liked about Jazz Fest than the current extravaganza in New Orleans. And the Russian River Jazz Festival in Guerneville each September offers a wonderful Northern California version of community and music.

It seems that every event strives to get bigger. How many people attend, or how much money is made, or how much is contributed to the designated charity becomes the measure of success. As an event grows, it attracts sponsors, gains advertising and publicity, and larger crowds. The events feed themselves, along with an ever-growing cadre of workers, promoters, and volunteers. Eventually, they lose their individuality as growth makes them just like any other big event.

The wine business knows all about getting bigger. Vineyards have continued to proliferate throughout California, Oregon, Washington and other parts of America. We may soon drown in the oncoming sea of bulk wine accumulating in tanks all over the country. The Napa Wine Auction has grown into an ostentatious ode to ego, and money. "Some of it goes to charity, you know." The ZAP tasting now requires two halls at Fort Mason, and still can't handle the crush of crowds clamoring for their zinfandel.

So, it was with great trepidation that Jake Lorenzo accepted an invitation to attend this year's Rhone Ranger tasting event. I was stunned at how comfortable the whole thing was. Lots of people attended, to be sure, but there was no crush of bodies against the tables. The din of voices ricocheting around the old barn of a building was bearable rather than mind numbing as it has been in the past. Winemakers and owners manned the tables, and were available to answer questions if necessary, but mostly they just poured.

There were viogniers, marsannes, carignanes, grenaches, syrahs, and petite syrahs. Most of them were well made, and Jake Lorenzo found a few of them to be thrilling. Kevin Hamel continues to make big, lush, age-worthy syrah. McRae from Washington State had a stable of elegant syrahs. Chuy liked the Jade Mountain syrah, and Jakelyn's mother thought the Foxen was pretty good. I tasted about 30 wines in a relaxed, comfortable setting over the course of 90 minutes. From my perspective it was a terrific event.

I don't know about the perspective of the Rhone Rangers. I mean, what good is a room full of Rhone Rangers if there aren't enough people for them to protect and serve? Rangers connote law and order in the face of wine crimes. After all, they helped save us from chardonnay. Maybe they had hoped for a crush of clamoring fans grappling for tastes of Rhone splendor. Perhaps they would have preferred teeming throngs fighting for tastes of viognier and marsanne. What they got was civilized. I liked it. In fact, I may go back again next year.

I suppose there is a lesson to be learned here, but Jake Lorenzo is a private eye, not a teacher. I can tell you this, when a big event turns out to be smaller than expected, it's always a good thing for the attendees. It's basic economics. At an event, the attendees are the demand, and the people putting on the event are the supply. Relax the demand, and the suppliers get nicer, friendlier, and cheaper.

In the wine business, wineries are the supply and consumers are the demand. Today, supply is getting way ahead of demand. Less demand means the wineries will get nicer, friendlier, and cheaper. A boom time's coming for consumers—and Jake Lorenzo is one. Bring it on. I'm ready.

A WILD HAIR IDEA

C'mon, Iggy, what the hell would Jake Lorenzo, private eye, do at a science convention."

"I told you, Jake," answered Dr. Iggy Calamari, "it's not a science convention at all. It's the Wild Hair Conference. Anyone with a wild hair idea can make a presentation. If your wine affirmative action plan isn't a wild hair idea, I'm not a scientist."

"It's just me blowing off steam," I say, "I haven't really figured it out yet."

"Well, son, you better get the mind waves bending, because tomorrow you'll be pitching your idea to a room full of the country's brightest wackos."

I'll tell you Jake Lorenzo's thinking on this one. I've known Iggy Calamari for more than fifteen years. He's a great scientist. Not only did he invent the wine-powered pacemaker, but he's also done research into all sorts of things, some wine related some not. Last year he almost killed me with a "research" eating binge in Belgium. Years before, I got a pretty bad sunburn testing out a theory of his. Iggy figured the minute quantities of lead ingested by wine drinkers from bottles containing lead capsules would protect us from harmful ultraviolet rays. After the test, as we sat drinking, Iggy commented on my discomfort. "It's a small sacrifice you make to further science. Stop whining and pass the pinot noir."

The thing about Iggy is he's crazy, but lots of the crazy things he talks about happen. Iggy projected the stock market crash. He predicted the widespread success of cellular telephones. Right now, among other things, he's working on a fusion formula that converts the power of splitting atoms into fuel for space missions. There's no doubt in my mind that within a few years, space ships won't be using fuel. They'll use fusion.

So, my detective side can't really pass up an opportunity to see Iggy at the Wild Hair Conference. Jake Lorenzo's got to rub elbows with the guys who rub elbows with Dr. Iggy Calamari. I've got to see and hear for myself what the current thinking is, when it's the country's weirdest scientists doing the thinking.

The next day we drive to San Francisco, and head to Union Square. Beneath the hip Farallon Restaurant is an Elk's Club. The Wild Hair Convention is held in the pool, where everyone is naked. When called, the presenters wrap a towel around themselves and walk to the podium. Applause is wet, sort of like seals clapping.

The Wild Hair ideas were certainly out there. Stuff like holographic projection cameras in convention sites, so three dimensional projections would appear in various locations simulating group attendance, when in fact, all the attendees were in different cities. Or how about rolls of saran wrap that tear like paper towels, instead of using a cutter? They had one guy who ran a small steam engine using the energy derived from kernels of corn being popped. Another lady had added Viagra to irrigation water to create corn that withstood gale force winds. It was fascinating, and a bit strange.

Iggy made an awesome presentation. His concept was rationed driving. Iggy said that traffic was slowly killing our ability to travel. Every family has two or three cars. The cars are getting bigger, unnecessarily. As Iggy put it, "SUV's in California? We need four wheel drive and lumpy, bumpy rides to scale the two-mile-an-hour, bumper-to-bumper rush hour traffic? If people won't use common sense, and use public transportation, then we've got to make private car usage less attractive."

Dr. Calamari's plan calls for rationing car drive time. Based on the same technology that allows for pre-paid phone calling cards, each person applies for and receives a designated amount of weekly drive time for their vehicle. A small computer chip in the vehicle is credited with that amount of time. Use it up, and the car won't start. People would have to ration their time. No more driving down to the store for a six-pack. Better to walk and save the drive time. Soccer moms, better start car-pooling, if they want to have enough time left on their cars to get to work. Take a bus to work once a week, and you'll get extra miles for that vacation you want to take.

There was a lot of debate, and complaining, and arguing, but Iggy had an answer for every devil's advocate. By the time he was done, I started thinking about how I could cut back on my car usage.

I was deep in thought, when from the podium Iggy introduced me as the next speaker. "My good friend Jake Lorenzo has a Wild Hair called Wine Affirmative Action. Please listen up to the good detective."

I'll tell you the truth. I'm not a great public speaker. But what I lack in professional ability, I make up for in passionate delivery. Basically, I told everyone that wine prices have gone beyond ridiculous. It's like everyone is making $80, and $100, and $500 bottles of wine. Of course, you can only buy one or two bottles, even if you have the money to afford them. It's a strange way to sell wine. Maybe, if we agreed that the wine was truly spectacular, year in and year out, with a long history of quality, like Chateau d'Yquem, it would be worth the money and aggravation. But these are wines with little history, with no track record, and no consensus as to quality.

Prices are based on what the market will bear, not quality in the bottle. Wineries say, "If Joe is getting $80 bucks, then mine should be at least $100." Marketing people think that if it's less than $60 a bottle, no one will buy it. "What about the working people?" asks Jake Lorenzo. "How much are you paying the guy who prunes those vines or picks those grapes? Can he afford to buy a bottle of your wine, this wine that he helped to make?"

Something is very wrong, if the people working at making the wine, can't afford to buy it given the money they're being paid to do the work.

Wine Affirmative Action addresses this problem. Wineries set aside 3% of their inventory for Affirmative Action. Field workers and working poor, the unemployed, and single mothers and fathers can apply for affirmative action. Based on need, the wineries distribute their wines to the qualified recipients...at cost. This enables a wide variety of people to drink these wines. The wineries get paid, so they don't lose money on the deal, (except for the lopsided profit), and it's only on 3% of the wine production.

This allows people to drink the wine who would otherwise never have the chance. If the recipients can't handle the idea of drinking a bottle of wine, the regular price of which could feed their family for a week, then let them sell the bottle at full price and keep the outrageous profit for themselves.

There are many benefits to this plan. It brings new drinkers into fine wine appreciation. It gives the common man and woman a chance to taste and comment on the quality of these expensive wonders. It doesn't cost the wineries much to finance.

The Wild Hair crowd loved the idea. Jake Lorenzo was feeling pretty good, but the good Dr. Calamari brought me back down to earth. "You have a way with dreamers, Jake, it's business people who don't understand you."